Aunt Phil's Trunk Volume Five

Teacher Guide

Bringing Alaska's history alive!

By
Laurel Downing Bill

Special credit and much appreciation to Nicole Cruz for her diligent efforts to create the best student workbook and teacher guide available for Alaska history studies.

Aunt Phil's Trunk LLC, Anchorage, Alaska
www.auntphilstrunk.com

Copyright © 2017 by Laurel Downing Bill.

All rights reserved. No part of this book may be used or reproduced in any manner whatsoever without written permission from the author, except in the case of brief quotations embodied in critical articles and reviews.

International Standard Book Number 978-1-940479-31-6
Printed and bound in the United States of America.

First Printing 2017
First Printing Second Edition 2018

Photo credits on the front cover, from top left: Native shaman with totem, Alaska State Library, Case and Draper Collection, ASL-P-39-782; Eskimo boy, Alaska State Library, Skinner Foundation, ASL-P44-11-002; Prospector, Alaska State Library, Skinner Foundation, ASL-P44-03-15; Athabascan woman, Anchorage Museum of History and Art, Crary–Henderson Collection, AMHA-b62-1-571; Gold miners, Alaska State Library, Harry T.Becker Collection, ASL-P67-052; Chilkoot Pass, Alaska State Library, Eric A. Hegg Collection, ASL-P124-04; Seal hunter, Alaska State Library, George A. Parks Collection, ASL-P240-210; Women mending boat, Alaska State Library, Rev. Samuel Spriggs Collection, ASL-P320-60; Teacher photo, Alaska State Library, J. Simpson MacKinnon Photo Collection, ASL-P14-073.

TABLE OF CONTENTS

Instructions *Aunt Phil's Trunk* Alaska History Curriculum	5
How to use this workbook at home	6
How to use this workbook for high school	7
How to use this workbook in the classroom	8
How to grade assignments	9
Rubric for Essay Questions	11
Rubric for Oral Presentations	12
Rubric for Enrichment Activities	12

UNIT 1: THE BIG YEAR

Lesson 1: The People's Governor	13
Lesson 2: Move the Capital	15
Lesson 3: First State Legislature	18
Lesson 4: From Forest to Flagpole	20
Review Lessons 1-4	22
Unit Test	26

UNIT 2: FIRST FIVE YEARS OF STATEHOOD

Lesson 5: Post Article Causes Concern	28
Lesson 6: Blue Canoes Make Debut	30
Lesson 7: The Lost Alaskans	33
Review Lessons 5-8	37
Unit Test	40

UNIT 3: EARTHQUAKE!

Lesson 8: Good Friday 1964	42
Lesson 9: Anchorage Hit Hard	45
Lesson 10: Wild Waves Bash Whittier	47
Lesson 11: Seawater Seeps into Portage	47
Lesson 12: Alaska Railroad Damaged	49
Lesson 13: Seward Burns	49
Lesson 14: Valdez Washed Away	49
Lesson 15: Chenega Destroyed	52
Lesson 16: Cordova And Other Small Towns	52
Lesson 17: Tidal Waves Overtake Kodiak	55
Lesson 18: Villages Near Kodiak in Ruins	55
Lesson 19: Alaskans Learn They're Not Alone	59
Lesson 20: Rebuilding Better Than Before	59
Review Lessons 8-20	64
Unit Test	68

TABLE OF CONTENTS

UNIT 4: ALASKA LAND IN DISPUTE
Lesson 21: Homesteaders Head North — 71
Lesson 22: Who Owns the Land? — 73
Lesson 23: Rock, Native Unity and Land Claims — 75
Lesson 24: Natives Must Prove Land Use — 78
Review Lessons 21-24 — 81
Unit Test — 85

UNIT 5: PRUDHOE BAY OIL
Lesson 25: Black Gold Found on North Slope — 87
Lesson 26: Deadhorse Rises in the Arctic — 89
Lesson 27: Plans For a Pipeline Progress — 91
Lesson 28: Pipeline Snakes Across Alaska — 93
Review Lessons 25-28 — 96
Unit Test — 100

UNIT 6: SOME HIGHLIGHTS
Lesson 29: Iceworm Revives Cordova — 102
Lesson 30: The Painting Pachyderm — 104
Lesson 31: Betty the Firetruck — 104
Lesson 32: A Great Race is Born — 106

UNIT 7: SOME LOW POINTS
Lesson 33: Cordova Burns — 110
Lesson 34: Floodwaters Fill Fairbanks — 112
Lesson 35: Congressmen Disappear — 114
Review Lessons 29-35 — 116
Unit Test — 121

MASS MURDER IN THE NORTH
(No Lessons for this section)

UNIT 9: 25 YEARS IN THE NEWS
Lesson 40: 1960s In the News — 125
Lesson 41: 1970s In the News — 127
Lesson 42: 1980s In the News — 129
Review Lessons 40-42 — 132
Unit Test — 134

Teacher notes — 136

Welcome to *Aunt Phil's Trunk Volume Five* Teacher Guide!

Read the chapters associated with each Unit. Then complete the lessons for that Unit to get a better understanding of Alaska's people and the events that helped shape Alaska's future.

I hope you enjoy your journey into Alaska's past from the years 1960 to 1984.

Laurel Downing Bill, author

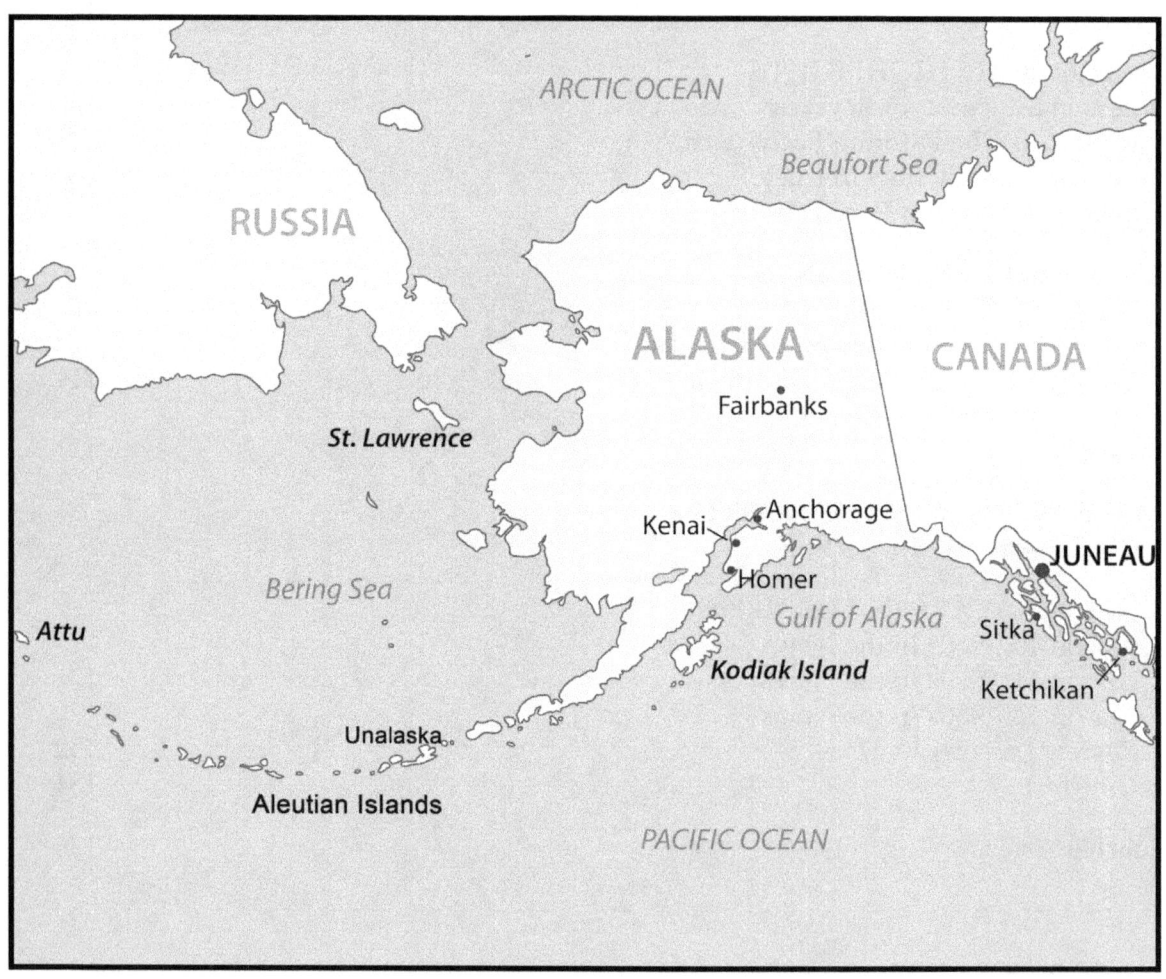

Instructions for using the Aunt Phil's Trunk Alaska History Curriculum

The *Aunt Phil's Trunk* Alaska History Curriculum is designed to be used in grades 4-8. High school students can use this curriculum, also, by taking advantage of the essay and enrichment activities throughout the book. The next few pages give further instruction on how to use this curriculum with middle school students, high school students and in classroom settings.

This curriculum can be taught in multiple grade levels by having your older students complete all reading, study guide work and enrichment activities independently. Students of all grade levels can participate in daily oral review by playing games like Jeopardy or Around the World.

This curriculum was developed so that students not only learn about Alaska's past, but they will have fun in the process. After every few lessons, they can test their knowledge through word scramble, word search and crossword puzzles.

Notes for parents with younger students:

Enrichment Activities occasionally direct your child to watch educational videos on YouTube.com or link to other Websites to learn more about the topic that they are reading about in the lesson. You may want to supervise younger children while they are using the Internet to be sure that they do not click on any inappropriate content. This also provides a good opportunity to discuss Internet safety with your child/children.

Chapters on historical murder cases:

Chapters 36-39 contain details about historical murder cases that may be too graphic for some students/classrooms. Teachers can elect to assign these chapters for extra reading. Please note that there are no workbook lessons for these chapters.

How to use this workbook at home

Aunt Phil's Trunk Alaska History Curriculum is designed to be used in grades 4-8. High school students can use this curriculum, also, by taking advantage of the essay and enrichment activities throughout the book. The next page gives further instruction on how to use this curriculum with high school students.

This curriculum can be taught in multiple grade levels by having your older students complete all reading, study guide work and enrichment activities independently. Students of all grade levels can participate in daily oral review by playing games like Jeopardy or Around the World.

For Middle School Students:

1. **Facts to Know:** Read this section in the study guide with your student(s) before reading the chapter to get familiar with new terms that they will encounter in the reading.

2. **Read the chapter:** Read one chapter aloud to your student(s) or have them read it aloud to you. Older students may want to read independently.

3. **Comprehension Questions:** Younger students may answer the comprehension questions orally or write down their answers in the study guide. Use these questions to test your student(s) comprehension of the chapter. Older students should answer all questions in written form.

4. **Discussion Questions:** Have your student(s) answer these questions in a few sentences orally. Come up with follow-up questions to test your student(s) understanding of the material. Older students may answer discussion questions in written essay form.

5. **Map Work:** Some chapters will contain a map activity for your student(s) to learn more about the geography of the region that they are learning about.

6. **Enrichment and Online References:** (Optional) Assign enrichment activities as you see fit. Many of the online references are from the Alaska Humanities Forum website (http://www.akhistorycourse.org). We highly recommend this website for additional information, project ideas, etc.

7. **Unit Review:** At the end of a unit, your student will complete Unit Review questions and word puzzles in the study guide. Students should review all the chapters in the unit before completing the review. Parents may want to assist younger students with the word puzzles.

8. **Unit Test:** (Optional) There is an optional test that you can administer to your student(s) after they have completed all the unit work.

How to use this workbook for high school

1. **Facts to Know:** Your student(s) should read this section in the study guide before reading the chapter to get familiar with new terms that they will encounter.

2. **Read the chapter:** Your student(s) can read aloud or independently.

3. **Comprehension Questions:** Use these questions to test your student(s) comprehension of the chapter. Have your high schoolers write out their answers in complete sentences.

4. **Discussion Questions:** Have your student(s) answer these questions in a few sentences orally or write out their answer in essay form.

5. **Map Work:** Some chapters will contain a map activity for your student(s) to learn more about the geography of the region that they are learning about.

6. **Enrichment and Online References:** Once your high schooler has completed all the reading and study guide material for the chapter, assign additional reading from the enrichment material using the online links or book lists. Encourage your student(s) to explore topics of interest to them.

Many of the online references are from the Alaska Humanities Forum website. We highly recommend this website for additional information, project ideas, etc.

7. **Unit Review:** At the end of a unit, your student will complete Unit Review questions and word puzzles in their study guide. Students should review all the chapters in the unit before completing the review.

8. **Unit Test:** (Optional) There is an optional test that you can administer to your student(s) after they have completed all the unit work.

9. **Oral Presentation:** (Optional) Assign a 5-minute oral presentation on any topic in the reading. Encourage your student(s) to utilize the additional books and online resources to supplement the information in the textbook. Set aside a classroom day for your student(s) to share their presentations.

10. **Historical Inquiry Project:** Your student(s) will choose a topic from the reading to learn more about and explore that topic through library visits, museum trips, visiting historical sites, etc.

Visit https://www.nhd.org/how-enter-contest for detailed information on how to put together a historical inquiry project. You may even want to have your students enter the national contest.

How to use this workbook in the classroom

Aunt Phil's Trunk Alaska History Curriculum was created for homeschooling families, but it also can work well in a co-op or classroom setting. Here are some suggestions on how to use this curriculum in a classroom setting. Use what works best for your classroom.

1. **Facts to Know:** The teacher introduces students to the Facts to Know to familiarize the students with terms that they will encounter in the chapter.

2. **Read the chapter:** The teacher can read the chapter aloud while the students follow along in the book. Students also may take turns reading aloud.

3. **Comprehension Questions:** The teacher uses these questions to test the students' comprehension of the chapter. Students should write out the answers in their study guide and the teacher can review the answers with the students in class.

4. **Discussion Questions:** The teacher chooses a few students to answer these questions orally during class. Alternatively, teachers can assign these questions to be completed in essay form individually and answers can be shared during class.

5. **Map Work:** Some chapters will contain a map activity for your students to learn more about the geography of the region that they are learning about. Have your students complete the activity independently.

6. **Enrichment and Online References:** Assign enrichment activities as you see fit.

7. **Daily Review:** Students should review the material for the current unit daily. You can do this by asking review questions orally. Playing review games like Jeopardy or Around the World is a fun way to get your students excited about the material.

8. **Unit Review:** At the end of a unit, your student will complete Unit Review questions and word puzzles in the study guide. Have students review all the unit chapters before completing.

9. **Unit Test:** (Optional) There is an optional test that you can administer to your students after they have completed all the unit work.

10. **Oral Presentation:** (Optional) Assign a 5-minute oral presentation on any topic in the reading. Encourage your students to utilize the additional books and online resources to supplement the information in the textbook. Set aside a classroom day for students to share their presentations.

11. **Historical Inquiry Project:** Your student(s) will choose a topic from the reading to learn more about and explore that topic through library visits, museum trips, visiting historical sites, etc.

Visit https://www.nhd.org/how-enter-contest for detailed information on how to put together a historical inquiry project. You may even want to have your students enter the national contest.

How to grade the assignments

Our rubric grids are designed to make it easy for you to grade your students' essays, oral presentations and enrichment activities. Encourage your students to look at the rubric grid before completing an assignment as a reminder of what an exemplary assignment should include.

You can mark grades for review questions, essay tests and extra credit assignments on the last page of each unit in the student workbook. Use these pages as a tool to help your students track their progress and improve their assignment grades.

Unit Review Questions

Students are given one point for each correct review and fill-in-the-blank question. Mark these points on the last page of each unit in the student workbook.

Essay Test Questions

Students will complete two or more essay questions at the end of each unit. These questions are designed to test your students' knowledge about the key topics of each unit. You can give a student up to 20 points for each essay.

Students are graded on a scale of 1-5 in four categories:

1) Understanding the topic
2) Answering all questions completely and accurately
3) Neatness and organization
4) Grammar, spelling and punctuation

Use the essay rubric grid on page 11 as a guide to give up to 5 points in each category for every essay. Mark these points for each essay on the last page of each Unit Review in the student workbook.

Word Puzzles

Word puzzles that appear at the end of the Unit Reviews count for 3 points, or you can give partial points if the student does not fill in the puzzle completely. Mark these points under the extra category on the last page of each Unit Review in the student workbook.

Enrichment Activities

Most lessons contain an enrichment activity for further research and interaction with the information in the lesson. You can make these optional or assign every activity as part of the lesson. You can use the provided rubric on page 12 to give up to 5 points for each assignment. Mark these points under the extra category on the last page of each Unit Review in the student workbook.

Oral Presentations

You have the option of assigning oral presentations on any topic from the unit as extra credit. If you choose to assign oral presentations, you can use the provided rubric to grade your student on content and presentation skills. Discuss what presentation skills you will be grading your student on before each presentation day.

Some examples of presentation skills you can grade on include:

- Eye contact with the audience
- Proper speaking volume
- Using correct posture
- Speaking clearly

Use the oral presentation rubric grid on page 12 as a guide to give up to 10 points. Mark these points under the extra category on the last page of each Unit Review in the student workbook.

Rubric for Essay Questions

	Beginning 1	Needs Improvement 2	Acceptable 3	Accomplished 4	Exemplary 5
Demonstrates Understanding of the topic	Student's work shows incomplete understanding of the topic	Student's work shows slight understanding of the topic	Student's work shows a basic understanding of the topic	Student's work shows complete understanding of the topic	Student's work demonstrates strong insight about the topic
Answered questions completely and accurately	Student's work did not address all of the questions	Student answered all of the questions with some accuracy	Student answered all questions with close to 100% accuracy	Student answered all questions with 100% accuracy	Student goes beyond the questions to demonstrate knowledge of the topic
Essay is neat and well organized	Student's work is sloppy and unorganized	Student's work is somewhat neat and organized	Student's essay is neat and somewhat organized	Student's work is well organized and neat	Student demonstrates extra care in organizing the essay and making it neat
Essay contains good grammar and spelling	Student's work is poorly written and hard to understand	Student's work contains some grammar, spelling and punctuation mistakes, but not enough to impede understanding	Student's work contains only 1 or 2 grammar, spelling or punctuation errors	Student's work contains no grammar, spelling or punctuation errors	Student's work is extremely well-written

Rubric for Oral Presentations

	Beginning 1	Needs Improvement 2	Acceptable 3	Accomplished 4	Exemplary 5
Preparation	Student did not prepare for the presentation	Student was somewhat prepared for the presentation	Student was prepared for the presentation and addressed the topic	Student was well-prepared for the presentation and addressed important points about the topic	Student prepared an excellent presentation that exhibited creativity and originality
Presentation Skills	Student demonstrated poor presentation skills (no eye contact, low volume, appears disinterested in the topic)	Student made some effort to demonstrate presentation skills (eye contact, spoke clearly, engaged audience, etc.)	Student demonstrated acceptable presentation skills (eye contact, spoke clearly, engaged audience, etc.)	Student demonstrated good presentation skills (eye contact, spoke clearly, engaged audience, etc.)	Student demonstrated strong presentation skills (eye contact, spoke clearly, engaged audience, etc.)

Rubric for Enrichment Activities

Beginning 1	Needs Improvement 2	Acceptable 3	Accomplished 4	Exemplary 5
Student's work is incomplete or inaccurate	Student's work is complete and somewhat inaccurate	Student completed the assignment with accuracy	Student's work is accurate, complete, neat and well-organized	Student demonstrates exceptional creativity or originality

UNIT 1: THE BIG YEAR

LESSON 1: THE PEOPLE'S GOVERNOR

FACTS TO KNOW

William A. Egan – Alaska's first elected governor and its first governor to be born in Alaska
Valdez – Birthplace of William Egan
Statehood – The status of being a state allowing for self-government

COMPREHENSION QUESTIONS

1) How did William Egan gain the tools needed to lead Alaska as it entered statehood? Consider what you learned about his past from the chapter. *He worked various jobs starting at the age of 10 to help support his family, such as: local cannery, shuttling tourists around his picturesque town and driving dump trucks for the Alaska Road Commission. He also learned to fly. His godfather, Anthony Dimond, sent copies of the Congressional Record back to Valdez for his constituents to read. His godson eagerly perused the documents and absorbed the nuances of politics with a passion. (Pages 12-22)*

2) William Egan suffered from glossophobia. What is it, and how did it affect him in his career? *Glossophobia is the fear of public speaking. He often practiced in front of a mirror to lessen the stress. A witness later said that during one of his speeches in the Legislature, even Republicans could be heard to mutter, "Come on, Bill, you can do it!" Even if public speaking was not his strong suit, members of both houses respected him. (Page 15)*

3) Why was Egan known as the "father of the constitution"? *When the 1955 Territorial Legislature decided to follow the precedent Tennessee had set in 1796 – drafting a constitution and electing congressmen as if it was already a state – they chose Egan as chairman of the Alaska Constitutional Convention. Egan presided over the 75-day convention at the University of Alaska at Fairbanks and became known as the father of the state's constitution. (Pages 15-16)*

4) When did Alaska officially become a state? Who made it official on this date? *U.S. President Dwight D. Eisenhower officially proclaimed Alaska a state with a stroke of his pen on Jan. 3, 1959, in Washington, D.C. (Pages 17-18)*

5) Why was William Egan admitted to the hospital just hours after he was sworn into office as Alaska's first elected governor? Who took his place as he recovered?
Egan had surgery to remove his gall bladder and a gallstone. The surgery was a success, but Egan suffered an acute pancreatic attack on Jan. 14. A four-hour operation removed a bowel obstruction. Lieutenant Governor Hugh Wade led the legislature as William Egan recovered. (Pages 18-19)

DISCUSSION QUESTION

(Discuss this question with your teacher or write your answer in essay form below. Use additional paper if necessary.)

Why do you think it was important for Alaska to achieve statehood?

_____
_____
_____
_____
_____
_____
_____
_____
_____
_____
_____
_____
_____
_____
_____
_____
_____
_____

ENRICHMENT ACTIVITY

Create a timeline of the life and career of William Egan beginning from his birth in 1914 to his return to duties after his illness on April 20, 1959.

LEARN MORE

Read more about Alaska's road to statehood by visiting
http://www.akhistorycourse.org/modern-alaska/statehood

UNIT 1: THE BIG YEAR

LESSON 2: MOVE THE CAPITAL

FACTS TO KNOW

Juneau – The capital city of Alaska
Alaska Bill/Civil Code – Provided that Alaska's capital would be in Juneau in 1900

COMPREHENSION QUESTIONS

1) What were some of the reasons that petitioners wanted to move the capital from Juneau?
Juneau is not centrally or conveniently located for most Alaskans. Unlike capitals in sister states, people can't reach Juneau via a road system. There are too many mountains, glaciers and rain forests in the way. Juneau is accessible only by boat or plane, providing the weather cooperates. (Pages 23-24)

2) Why did some want to move the capital to Big Lake?
Some of the advantages were: 1. Level and rolling land with good drainage. 2. A good road system with prospects of better. 3. Alaska Railroad and airport facilities that can be enlarged. 4. Ideal weather conditions for health and flying. 5. Plenty of land, property values low. 6. Safe distance from military target, in case of nuclear warfare. 7. Big Lake and Mt. McKinley recreational areas, Matanuska Valley farm products and Anchorage culture only a short distance away. (Pages 24-25)

3) How did Juneau become Alaska's capital?
The discovery of gold deposits in the 1880s in the area that became Juneau caused that town to grow in population, influence and accommodations. Lawyers in Juneau began pressuring Congress to pass a bill that would move Alaska's seat of government to Juneau, stating the town now was the largest city in Alaska, had become an established mining town and had a promising future. U.S. President William McKinley signed the Alaska Bill, or Civil Code, into law on June 6, 1900, which provided that the temporary seat of government would be established at Juneau. (Pages 25-26)

4) What was Alaska's first legislative session in 1913 like? Where did the first legislators meet? How did the legislators travel there?
Alaska's first legislative session, consisting of eight senators and 15 of 16 elected representatives, met in the Elks Hall in Juneau for their first gathering on March 3, 1913. The federal government paid them $15 per day (about $360 in today's dollars) and .15 per

mile, which came to $600-$700 for the Nome fellows who traveled by dog teams (around $16,400 in 2015 dollars). Many of the lawmakers traveled by sled dogs. (Pages 28-29)

5) Name another area that was considered for Alaska's capital. What happened?
Following Alaska's official entry as the 49th state on Jan. 3, 1959, a petition immediately began circulating to move the capital. On Aug. 9, 1960, voters turned down Initiative Proposal No. 1 to move the capital from Juneau to the Cook Inlet Railbelt area with 18,856 voting yes and 23,972 voting no. (Page 30)

DISCUSSION QUESTION

(Discuss this question with your teacher or write your answer in essay form below. Use additional paper if necessary.)

What are some reasons that the issue of moving the capital died in the new state legislature?

_____
_____
_____
_____
_____
_____
_____
_____
_____
_____
_____
_____
_____
_____
_____
_____
_____
_____
_____

LEARN MORE

Read more about the votes to move the capital by visiting
http://www.akhistorycourse.org/governing-alaska/capitol-move-ballot-measures

MAP ACTIVITY

Locate the following cities on the map below:

1) Juneau   2) Big Lake   3) Nome   4) Fairbanks   5) Willow

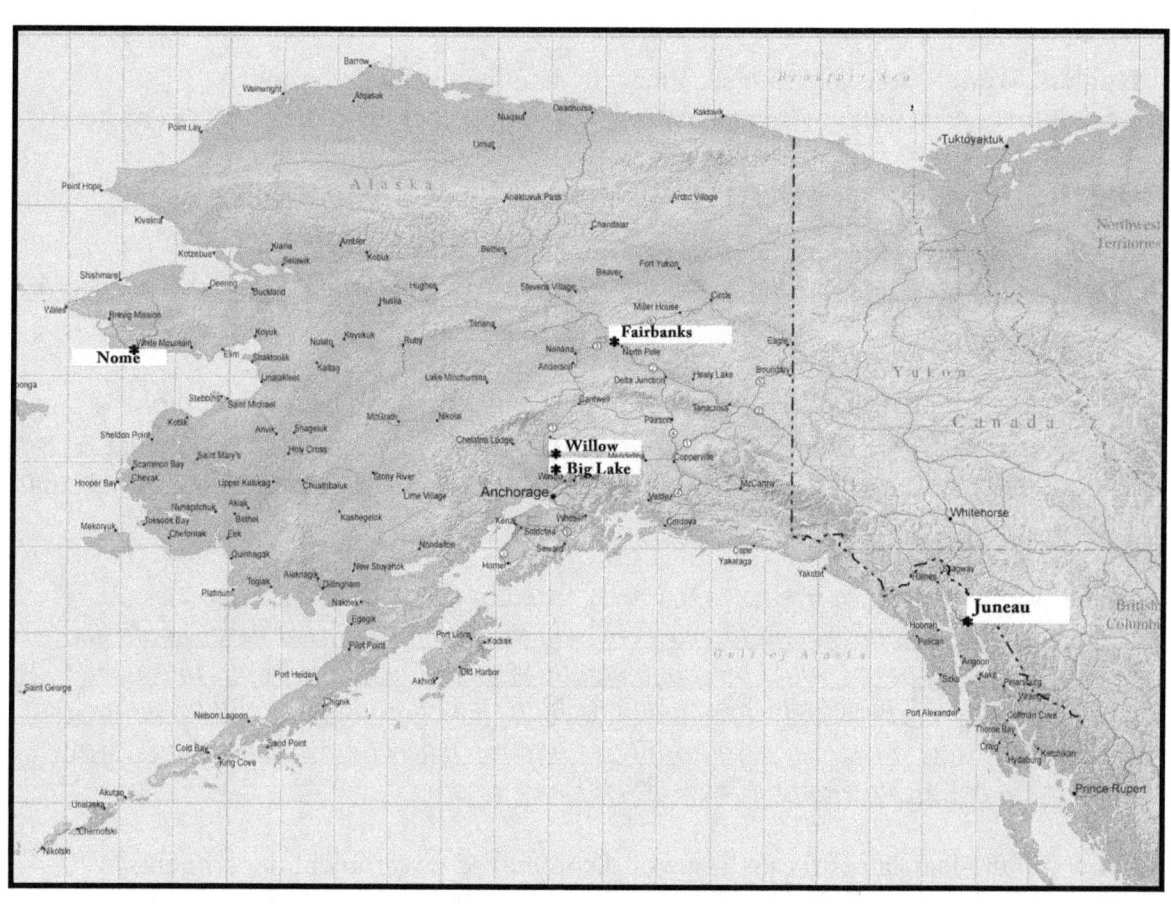

UNIT 1: THE BIG YEAR

LESSON 3: FIRST STATE LEGISLATURE

FACTS TO KNOW

Hugh J. Wade – Alaska's first secretary of state/lieutenant governor
Legislator – A member of an elected group who together have the power to make laws

COMPREHENSION QUESTIONS

1) Who led the first state legislature when it began in 1959? Why?
Acting Gov. Hugh Wade led the legislature because Gov. William Egan was recovering from abdominal surgery. (Pages 37-38)

2) What were some of the tasks that the first Alaska lawmakers had to accomplish?
The lawmakers had to create dozens of bills to build the infrastructure necessary to run the nation's newest state. They had to sort out a disorganized government and pass a state budget. (Pages 38-42)

3) What were some of the obstacles that they faced in accomplishing these tasks?
They began their business amid forecasts by doomsayers that Alaska never could survive as a state and never would be economically viable. People were split into numerous local factions over where highways should be built, how boroughs should be set up and how the state would take over responsibilities that the federal government had always taken care of before statehood. (Pages 38-39)

4) How did the legislators fix the issue of disorganized government departments?
Lawmakers passed the Statehood Organization Act that created 12 executive departments: administration, law, revenue, health and welfare, labor, commerce, military affairs, natural resources, public safety, public works, education and fish and game. (Pages 40-41)

5) What other accomplishments did the new lawmakers achieve? *Other accomplishments during this session included: establishing the Alaska Public Employees' Retirement System; prohibiting commercial fish traps; passing the Alaska Lands Act; creating the seal of the state; setting the drinking age at 21; permitting women serving as waitresses in restaurants to serve alcohol; establishing numerous professional licensing boards; and establishing a minimum wage of $1.50 per hour. (Page 42)* **Teacher's Note: You may want to tell students that $1.50 per hour minimum wage in 1959 equates to $12.65 in 2017.**

DISCUSSION QUESTION

(Discuss this question with your teacher or write your answer in essay form below. Use additional paper if necessary.)

What qualifications did Hugh Wade have to become Alaska's first secretary of state and acting governor as William Egan recovered from surgery?

_____
_____
_____
_____
_____
_____
_____
_____
_____
_____
_____
_____
_____
_____
_____
_____
_____
_____
_____

ENRICHMENT ACTIVITY

Imagine that you are the governor of a brand-new state. Write a list of all the important things that you and your team need to accomplish to set up the state. Look back at the chapter if you need help coming up with ideas. What laws need to be passed? What organizations need to be in place?

(Note to Teacher: If you are in a classroom setting, you can make this a group project. Split the students into groups, and then have each group appoint a governor to lead the discussion, a second-in-command and a secretary to take notes. Each governor will be responsible for presenting the results of the group's meeting to the class.)

LEARN MORE

Read about the legislative branch by visiting
http://www.akhistorycourse.org/governing-alaska/the-legislative-branch

UNIT 1: THE BIG YEAR

LESSON 4: FROM FOREST TO FLAGPOLE

FACTS TO KNOW

Prince of Wales Island – Island in the Southeast Alaska panhandle where the spruce tree grew that would be sent to Anchorage

Ketchikan – A small town located along the Tongass Narrows on Revillagigedo Island in Southeast Alaska

Anchorage – Largest city in Alaska, located in southcentral, where the largest flagpole stood

George H. Byer – Former Anchorage mayor and chairman of the Anchorage Parks and Recreation Commission in 1970

COMPREHENSION QUESTIONS

1) Why did many Americans refer to Alaska as "Seward's Ice Box" in the 1800s?
Secretary of State William Seward finalized the purchase of Alaska from the Russians on March 30, 1867. Most Americans at the time thought Alaska unimportant and referred to it as "Seward's Ice Box" because they thought it a useless, frozen land. (Page 47)

2) How did a spruce tree from Prince of Wales Island become a symbol of importance to Alaska in 1959?
After the spruce tree was sent to Alaska's largest city, it became the tallest flagpole in the newest state and displayed the new 49-star flag at Anchorage City Hall in 1959. (Page 47)

3) Why did many people think the spruce tree was a joke?
One article appearing in the Anchorage Daily News on Sept. 10, 1959, reported that a man from Ketchikan claimed the huge pole, which measured 140 feet long, was selected because people in Ketchikan didn't think the folks in Anchorage would know what to do with it. "The theory was that it was too big a project even for 'Big Anchorage' to complete," the article stated. Some suggested their Southeast neighbors had sent Alaska's largest city a huge headache. (Pages 47-49)

4) What did George Byer say in a letter to the newspapers about the "prank"?
The "gag" actually originated in Anchorage, Byer said in his letter dated Dec. 4, 1970. "... I thought it would be a nice gesture of one All-American City to another to do a real

patriotic deed," he wrote. "And in view of statehood it would be great to have the tallest flagpole in the largest state in the biggest city to fly the newest 49th state flag." (Pages 48-49)

5) How did townspeople celebrate their new flagpole in 1959? What additional improvements were made to it?
Townspeople attended a colorful ceremony on the Anchorage City Hall lawn to dedicate the flagpole on Labor Day, Sept. 8. More than 100 people gathered on Fourth Avenue to watch as Gov. William A. Egan unveiled a plaque on the pole with a quote by Daniel Webster. Within a year of the dedication ceremony, construction began on a crown to top the tallest natural flagpole in the new state – a stainless steel globe. Volunteers throughout Anchorage painted the pole and the Garden Club decorated the area for the globe's dedication. (Pages 51-53)

DISCUSSION QUESTION

(Discuss this question with your teacher or write your answer in essay form below. Use additional paper if necessary.)

What surprises were found regarding this flagpole years after it was raised?

_____
_____
_____
_____
_____
_____
_____
_____
_____
_____
_____
_____
_____
_____
_____
_____
_____
_____

TIME TO REVIEW

Review Chapters 1-4 of your book before moving on to the Unit Review. See how many questions you can answer without looking at your book.

UNIT 1: THE BIG YEAR

REVIEW LESSONS 1-4

Write down what you remember about:

William A. Egan – *Alaska's first elected governor and its first governor to be born in Alaska*

Valdez – *Birthplace of William Egan*

Statehood – *The status of being a state allowing for self-government*

Juneau – *The capital city of Alaska*

Alaska Bill/Civil Code – *Provided that Alaska's capital would be in Juneau in 1900*

Hugh J. Wade – *Alaska's first secretary of state/lieutenant governor*

Legislator – *A member of an elected group who together have the power to make laws*

Prince of Wales Island – *Island in the Alaska panhandle where the spruce tree grew that would be sent to Anchorage*

Ketchikan – *A small town located along the Tongass Narrows on Revillagigedo Island in Southeast Alaska*

Anchorage – *Largest city in Alaska, located in Southcentral, where the largest flagpole stood*

George H. Byer – *Former Anchorage mayor and chairman of the Anchorage Parks and Recreation Commission in 1970*

Fill in the blanks:

1) After his father was killed in an *avalance*, *William Egan* was attending school and working in a local *cannery* by the age of 10. Since there were no restrictions on *driver's ages* at the time, the lad also learned to *drive* and began *shuttling tourists* around his town during summers. By 14, he was *driving dump trucks* for the Alaska Road Commission.

2) He also learned to fly and caught the attention of *Robert "Bob" Campbell Reeve*, who arrived in his hometown of *Valdez* in 1932.

3) Although *William Egan* suffered from a fear of *public speaking*, he was chosen chairman and presided over the *Alaska Constitutional Convention* at the University of Alaska Fairbanks from November 1955 to February 1956.

4) Many people wanted to move the capital from *Juneau* because it is not *centrally or conveniently* located for most Alaskans. Unlike capitals in sister states, people can't reach *Juneau* via a road system. There are too many *mountains, glaciers and rain forests* in the way. It is accessible only by *boat or plane*, providing the weather cooperates.

5) The discovery of gold deposits in the 1880s in the area that became *Juneau* caused that town to grow in *population, influence and accommodations*. A need also grew to settle boundary disputes, contracts, payments and other legal matters that necessitated travel to *Sikta* to see a judge. Lawyers in *Juneau* began pressuring Congress to pass a bill that would move Alaska's seat of government to their city.

6) The first Alaska State *Legislature* met on Jan. 26, 1959, in the *Juneau Elks Hall*. It was led by *Acting Governor Hugh Wade* because William Egan was recovering from *abdominal surgery.*

7) Alaska's *legislators/lawmakers* rolled up their sleeves and began the task of creating dozens of *bills* to build the infrastructure necessary to run the nation's newest *state*. And they began their business amid forecasts by doomsayers that Alaska never could survive as a state and never would be *economically* viable.

8) The lawmakers accomplished many things during their first session such as: _organizing departments; creating a court system; passing a state budget; passing the Alaska Lands Act; creating the seal of the state; setting the drinking age at 21; permitting women serving as waitresses in restaurants to serve alcohol; and establishing a minimum wage of $1.50 per hour._

9) A _small spruce tree_ that began life on Prince of Wales Island in the mid-1700s found its way to _Anchorage_ when Alaska became America's 49th state. This Southeast sapling held no importance when Secretary of State _William Seward_ finalized the purchase of Alaska from the _Russians_ on March 30, 1867. And most Americans at the time thought Alaska unimportant, as well, and referred to it as "_Seward's Ice Box._"

10) It became the tallest _flagpole_ in the new state and displayed the new _49-star flag_ at _Anchorage_ City Hall in 1959. Some suggest it was a _prank_ originated by people in Ketchikan. According to an article in the _Anchorage_ Daily News, "The theory was that it was too big a project even for 'Big _Anchorage_' to complete," the article stated.

A young William "Bill" Egan became known for discussing issues and engaging in political debates at the Pinzon Bar in Valdez, seen here in the early 1930s.

Important People in the Big Year
Word Scramble Puzzle Key
Unscramble the words below

#	Scrambled	Answer	Clue
1.	almiiwl agne	william egan	First elected Alaska governor
2.	sneret negnriug	ernest gruening	One-time Alaska territorial governor elected to U.S. Senate
3.	dwarde elttarbt	edward bartlett	One of two U.S. senators that Alaskans first elected to U.S. Senate
4.	parlh vrries	ralph rivers	Alaskans chose him as first elected Representative to U.S. House
5.	wihdgt ewsoieenrh	dwight eisenhower	U.S. President who signed Alaska Statehood Bill in January 1959
6.	hhgu dwae	hugh wade	Alaska's first secretary of state/lieutenant governor
7.	foldy inuretg	floyd guertin	Alaska's first commissioner of Administration
8.	leicc nlotob	**cecil bolton**	Raised the first 49-star national flag at Anchorage City Hall on July 4, 1959
9.	ewnarr orlyat	warren taylor	First Speaker of the House in Alaska's first state legislature
10.	llbeu bensett	buell nesbett	Alaska's first chief justice on new state Supreme Court

UNIT 1: THE BIG YEAR

UNIT TEST

Choose *two* of the following questions to answer in paragraph form. Use as much detail as possible to completely answer the question.

1) Write a brief summary of notable events in the life of William Egan.

2) Why did some people want to move the capital of Alaska from Juneau? Why did others want to keep the capital in Juneau? Name at least two cities that were considered as potential capitals.

3) Who led the first state legislature? Why? What tasks did this first legislature accomplish during its first year?

4) How did a spruce tree from Prince of Wales Island become an important symbol in Alaska? Why did some consider this a prank?

TEACHER NOTES ABOUT THIS UNIT

UNIT 2: FIRST FIVE YEARS OF STATEHOOD

LESSON 5: POST ARTICLE CAUSES CONCERN

FACTS TO KNOW

Saturday Evening Post – Magazine that published an article portraying Alaska's economy in a negative light
Rebuttal – Argument or contradiction
Lester Bronson – Nome senator who thought Alaska was better off as a state
Bob DeArmond – Thought statehood for Alaska was a bad idea

COMPREHENSION QUESTIONS

1) Why did the Saturday Evening Post article titled "Alaska: Can it survive as a state?" cause concern? Summarize what the article stated.
It did not portray Alaska's economy in a positive light. Reporter Schulman stated that Alaska was suffering from a "severely sick economy" that was being supported by federal dollars. He ended the unflattering piece by saying that if the natural resources did not pan out, Alaska would "remain an invalid ward of the Federal Government." (Page 58)

2) What were some of the rebuttals to the article?
"A continually increasing number of new and old Alaskans could have provided Mr. Schulman with a ready answer to his question," Alaska Gov. William A. Egan wrote in a telegram to the Post. "Yes, Alaska not only will survive but will thrive as a state." State Sen. Lester Bronson, D-Nome, said he thought Alaska was much better off as a state. "I don't know what the man expects from a state just out of its diapers," Bronson said in an Anchorage Daily News rebuttal. (Pages 59-60)

3) Where did roughly 60 percent of the money flowing into Alaska in 1963 come from?
About 60 percent of the money flowing into the new state in its infancy came from federal transition grants to help Alaska move from federal control to independency. (Page 60)

4) What were some of the signs that Alaska was becoming self-sufficient in 1963?
The gross volume of business had almost doubled. Per capita income was highest in the nation, increasing by 7.5 percent in 1963 alone. The state's first producing oil field on the Kenai Peninsula was developed. The Marine Highway System was becoming a reality. The tourist industry was booming. And fishing remained one of the mainstays of the state's economy. (Page 60)

5) What were some of the advantages of statehood according to most Alaskans?
Instead of 54 separate federal agencies and commissions running the government, Alaska now controlled its own destiny. Alaskans no longer had "pinstriped bureaucrats" in Washington, D.C., making decisions on their behalf. They had two elected senators and a representative in Congress who had their best interests at heart. (Page 62)

DISCUSSION QUESTION

(Discuss this question with your teacher or write your answer in essay form below. Use additional paper if necessary.)

Name one industry that Alaska relied upon in its early years of statehood.

ENRICHMENT ACTIVITY

Search for an article in your local newspaper or a magazine that includes a strong opinion on any topic that interests you. What rebuttals could you make to the writer of the article? Do further research on the topic if necessary. Write a short rebuttal and present it to your teacher.

LEARN MORE

Read more about Alaska's expanding economy by visiting
http://www.akhistorycourse.org/southcentral-alaska/1930-1970-the-expanding-economy

UNIT 2: FIRST FIVE YEARS OF STATEHOOD

LESSON 6: BLUE CANOES MAKE DEBUT

FACTS TO KNOW

Richard Downing – Alaska's first commissioner of public works and early proponent of the Alaska Marine Highway System
Alaska Marine Highway System – Passenger-car ferry system created after statehood
M/V Malaspina – The first ferry launched in the Alaska Marine Highway System in 1963

COMPREHENSION QUESTIONS

1) Describe the first modern-day ferry system that began in 1949.
The genesis of the modern ferry system began in 1949 when Haines residents Steve Homer and Ray Gelotte founded the Chilkoot Motorship Lines. The men purchased and converted a surplus World War II LCT-Mark VI landing craft from the U.S. Navy and christened it the M/V Chilkoot. The vessel had a day lounge, bathrooms, a galley and crew quarters. (Page 65)

2) What was the "Blue Canoe"?
The Chilkat was dubbed the "Blue Canoe." It was 99 feet long, but could carry 59 passengers and 15 vehicles. Built by J.M. Martinac Shipbuilding Co. of Tacoma, Wash., it had a distinct bow ramp that allowed it to load from a beach as well as a dock. The ship was painted with the blue and gold of Alaska's flag. (Page 66)

3) Why did some people call the idea of the Alaska Marine Highway System "Downing's Folly"?
Public Works Commissioner Richard Downing wanted to create a marine highway that would serve and connect the communites of Southeast Alaska. Controversy surrounded the idea of the ferry system from the beginning. The author of this Alaska history series, Laurel Downing Bill, remembers some people calling the proposed ferry system "Downing's Folly" at the time (commissioner Downing was her father) – perhaps because much of Alaska's population did not live in Southeast and didn't understand the importance of connecting the communities on the Panhandle. Some may have thought the price too high to pay. Others saw it as a crazy idea that never would pay for itself. (Page 67)

4) What did Public Works Commissioner Downing do to prepare for the new ferry system?
Commissioner Downing consulted with experts in both Canada and the United States, which resulted in the "Study and Report on the Alaska Ferry System of February 1961," according to a newspaper article in the Juneau Empire. Downing acquired as much information as possible to make sure the ferry system would be practical, economical and of the most benefit to the people it would serve. (Pages 67-68)

5) What did Governor William Egan say about the Alaska Marine Highway System after his wife Neva, christened *M/V Malaspina*, the first ship in the new fleet?
When the ship slid down rails into the water, Gov. Egan said it was "perhaps the most important and permanent achievement for Alaska since statehood." (Page 68)

DISCUSSION QUESTION

(Discuss this question with your teacher or write your answer in essay form below. Use additional paper if necessary.)

How did the Alaska Marine Highway improve the quality of life for many Alaskans?

LEARN MORE

Learn more about marine transportation in Alaska by visiting
http://www.akhistorycourse.org/americas-territory/marine-transportation

MAP ACTIVITY

Using pages 74-78 of your textbook, mark the following stops along the Alaska Marine Highway System from Prince Rupert, British Columbia.

1) Ketchikan 2) Wrangell 3) Petersburg 4) Sitka 5) Juneau 6) Haines 7) Skagway

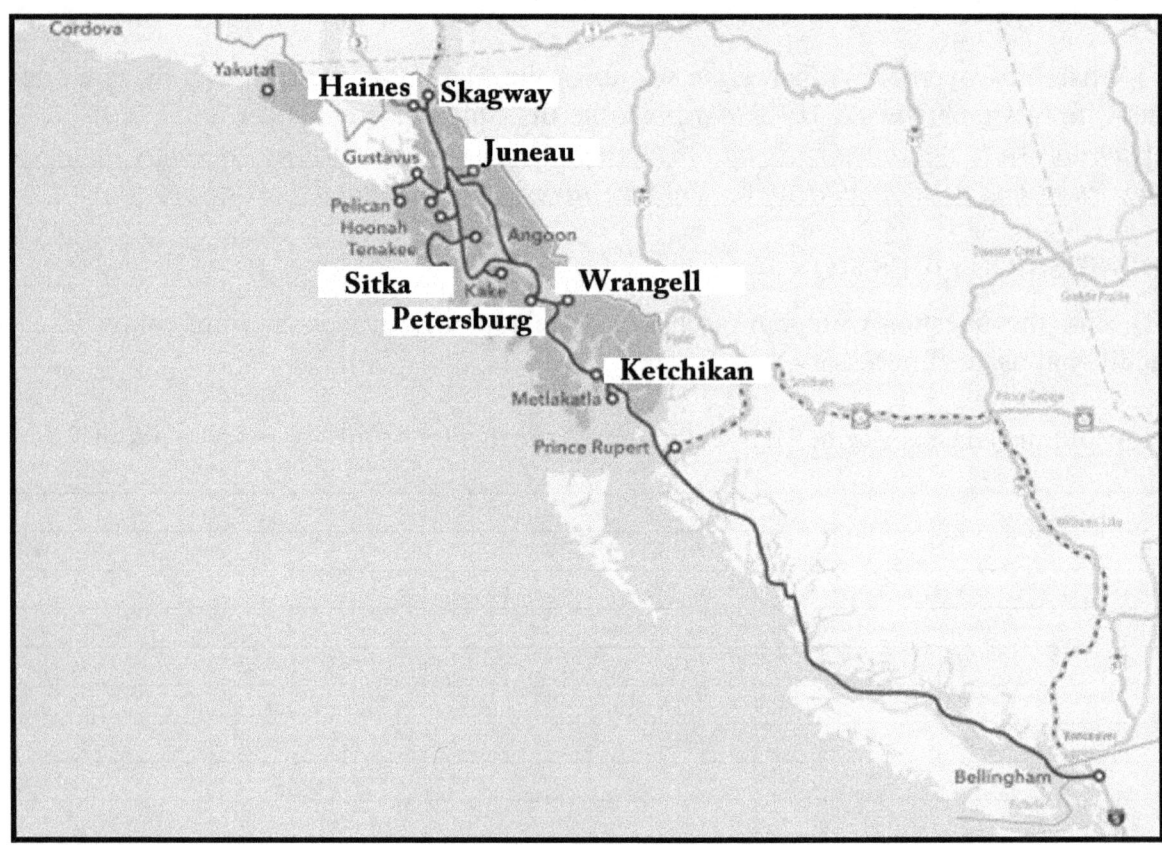

UNIT 2: FIRST FIVE YEARS OF STATEHOOD

LESSON 7: THE LOST ALASKANS

FACTS TO KNOW

Dr. Henry Waldo Coe – Founder of Morningside Hospital

Morningside Hospital – Mental health institution in Oregon where Alaskans deemed mentally ill were sent prior to the 1960s

Alaska Mental Health Enabling Act – Provided funding for Alaska's mental health care system

COMPREHENSION QUESTIONS

1) Who were the "Lost Alaskans" described in the chapter?
Prior to the 1956 Alaska Mental Health Enabling Act, those with mental illness in Alaska were shipped off to Morningside Hospital in Portland, Ore. – and most families never heard from their loved ones again. They became known as "The Lost Alaskans." (Page 79)

2) What was the procedure for determining mental illness in the early 1900s? How were those who were determined to be mentally ill treated?
At the time, mental illness was considered a crime and Alaskan adults and children were arrested. The procedure for determining mental illness was rather simple. A person said to be mentally ill was brought before a jury of six people who would rule him sane or insane. If he was found insane, he then was sent to jail until his release or transfer to Morningside Hospital in Oregon. Nowhere in this process was a medical or psychiatric examination required. (Pages 79-80)

3) Why did missionaries in Anvik send James Ebana to Morningside? What happened to him?
Apparently, missionaries at the Church Christ Mission in Anvik arranged to have James Ebana, then 17, sent to Morningside after he had a seizure in 1932. Like many people sent to the facility, Ebana's family never knew what happened to him after he left Anvik. The young man's death certificate stated he died of "Tuberculosis of the Lungs" in 1942, according to records at Morningside. (Pages 81-82)

4) What deficiencies were found during government investigations into Morningside's practices?
The investigations found widespread deficiencies in the program, including financial abuse by the Coe family. Investigators learned the family was subverting money intended for patient care to personal gain, including trips to South Africa and Mexico. They also

found the Coes had used patient labor for building and maintenance of the facility under the guise of occupational therapy, according to Morningside's Website. (Pages 82-83)

5) Why did some oppose the Alaska Mental Health Bill proposed to Congress in 1956? *The bill became the focus of major political controversy after opponents nicknamed it the "Siberia Bill" and claimed it was part of a Communist plot to institutionalize and brainwash Americans. Anticommunist groups said that the commitment language in the bill "takes away all of the rights of the American citizen to ask for a jury trial and protect him[self]. (Pages 84-85)*

6) How did the Alaska Mental Health Enabling Act change the mental health care system? *Language in the act provided funding for Alaska's mental health care system through lands allocated to a mental health trust. Although politicians later transferred most of the valuable land to state agencies and private individuals, the legal system ruled their actions illegal and a reconstituted mental health trust was established in the mid-1980s. (Page 86)*

DISCUSSION QUESTION

(Discuss this question with your teacher or write your answer in essay form below. Use additional paper if necessary.)

Do you think that Dr. Henry Coe should have been charged with a crime? Why or why not?

_____
_____
_____
_____
_____
_____
_____
_____
_____
_____
_____
_____
_____
_____

TIME TO REVIEW

Review Chapters 5-7 of your book before moving on the Unit Review. See how many questions you can answer without looking at your book.

Headlines First Five Years
Word Search Puzzle Key
Find the words listed below

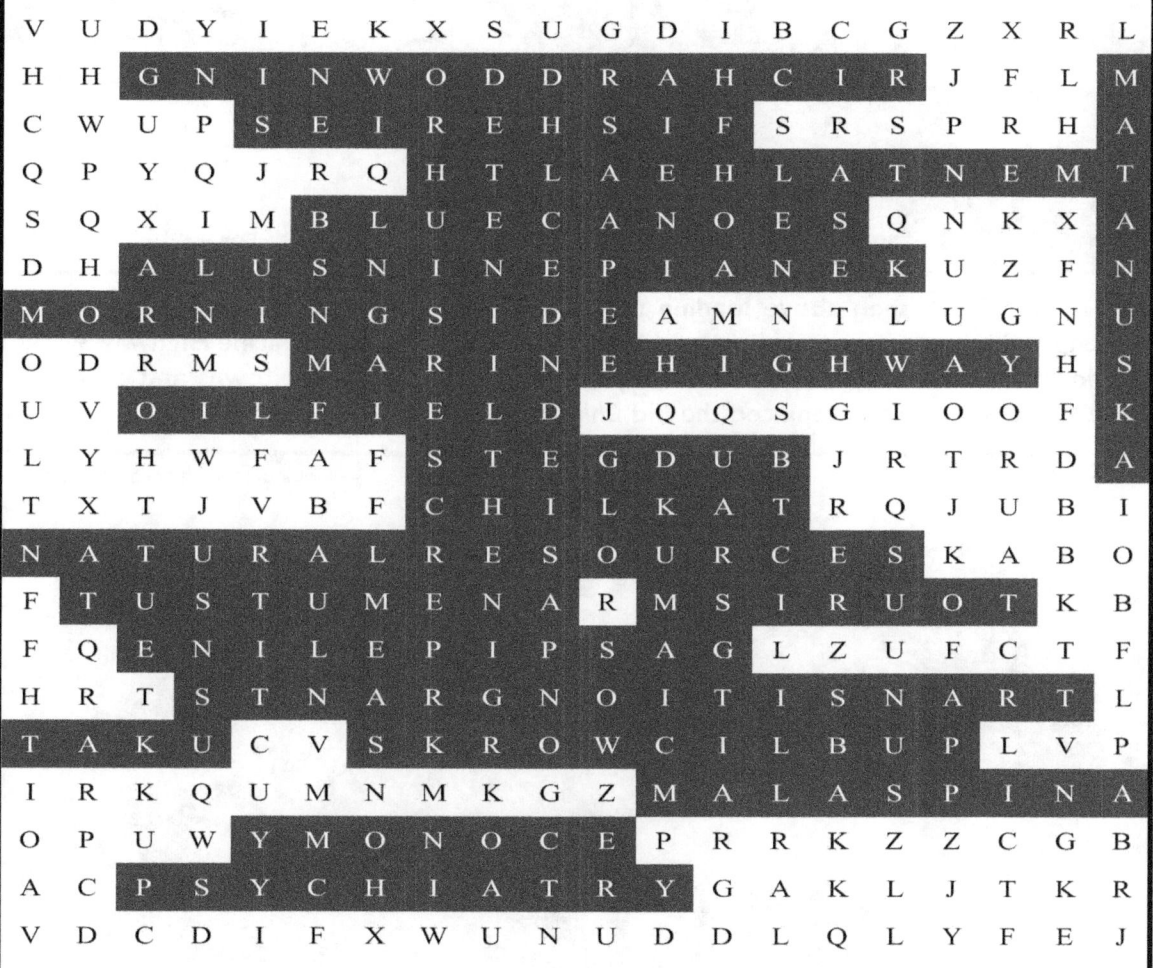

ECONOMY	CHILKAT	TRANSITION GRANTS
FISHERIES	TOURISM	OIL FIELD
BUDGETS	PUBLIC WORKS	RICHARD DOWNING
MARINE HIGHWAY	KENAI PENINSULA	GAS PIPELINE
MALASPINA	BLUE CANOES	NATURAL RESOURCES
TAKU	MATANUSKA	TUSTUMENA
MORNINGSIDE	MENTAL HEALTH	PSYCHIATRY

The *M/V Chilkoot*, seen above loading up in Juneau in 1950, could haul 13 cars and 20 passengers between Juneau, Haines and Skagway. Once the Alaska Marine Highway System was formed in the 1960s, docks and ramps were built in Southeast towns and eventually *M/V Chilkat,* seen below, replaced the old *Chilkoot*.

UNIT 2: FIRST FIVE YEARS OF STATEHOOD

REVIEW LESSONS 5-7

Write down what you remember about:

Saturday Evening Post – *Magazine that published an article portraying Alaska's economy in a negative light*

Rebuttal – *Argument or contradiction*

Lester Bronson – *Nome senator who thought Alaska was better off as a state*

Bob DeArmond – *Thought statehood for Alaska was a bad idea*

Richard Downing – *Alaska's first commissioner of public works and early proponent of the Alaska Marine Highway System*

Alaska Marine Highway System – *Passenger-car ferry system created after statehood*

M/V Malaspina – *The first ferry launched in the Alaska Marine Highway System in 1963*

Dr. Henry Waldo Coe – *Founder of Morningside Hospital*

Morningside Hospital – *Mental health institution in Oregon where Alaskans deemed mentally ill were sent prior to the 1960s*

Alaska Mental Health Enabling Act – *Provided funding for Alaska's mental health care system*

Fill in the blanks:

1) Many were stunned when an article in The *Saturday Evening Post* titled "Alaska: Can it survive as a state?" hit national newsstands October 1963. It did not portray Alaska's *economy* in a positive light.

2) The man who wrote the Post article, *Robert Schulman*, concluded that Alaska was suffering from a "severely sick *economy*" that was being supported by *federal dollars*. He ended the unflattering piece by saying that if the *natural resources* did not pan out, Alaska would "remain an invalid ward of *the Federal Government*."

3) That Post article unleashed a barrage of *rebuttal* articles and statements from Alaskans. "A continually increasing number of new and old Alaskans could have provided Mr. *Schulman* with a ready answer to his question," Alaska Gov. *William A. Egan* wrote in a telegram to the Post. "Yes, Alaska not only will survive but will *thrive* as a state."

4) Gov. *William A. Egan* appointed *Richard A. Downing* as the state's first commissioner of Public Works, and *Downing* made creating a *passenger-car ferry* system a priority. In January 1963, Southeasterners saw their dream of a *highway* that could connect their island-bound towns with the outside world become a reality with the maiden voyage of the *M/V Malaspina*, the first ferry of the *Alaska Marine Highway.*

5) The author of this Alaska history series, *Laurel Downing Bill*, remembers some people calling the proposed ferry system "*Downing*'s Folly" at the time – Alaska Public Works Commissioner *Richard A. Downing* was her father. Perhaps they said that because much of Alaska's population did not live in *Southeast Alaska* and they didn't understand the importance of connecting the communities on the *Panhandle*. Some may have thought the price too *high to pay*.

6) Gov. Egan said the *Alaska Marine Highway* was "perhaps the most *important and permanent achievement* for Alaska since statehood."

7) Prior to the 1956 *Alaska Mental Health Enabling Act*, those with mental illness were shipped off to *Morningside Hospital in Portland, Oregon* – and most families never heard from their loved ones again. They became known as "*The Lost Alaskans*."

8) At the time, mental illness was considered a *crime* and Alaskan adults and children were *arrested, convicted of insanity* and sent by the federal government via dog teams, trains and ships to live at *Morningside Hospital*.

9) Alaska only had one non-*voting* delegate in Congress in the mid-1950s – *E.L. "Bob" Bartlett*. He wrote H.R. 6376, the Alaska *Mental Health* Bill. It received bipartisan support and passed unanimously in January 1956. The bill became the focus of major political controversy after opponents nicknamed it the "*Siberia Bill*" and claimed it was part of a Communist plot to *institutionalize and brainwash* Americans.

10) The *Alaska Mental Health Enabling Act* provided funding for Alaska's mental health care system through *lands* allocated to a mental health trust. Republican Sen. Barry Goldwater helped craft the bill without the *commitment* provisions that had been the target of such intense opposition.

Courtesy Alaska State Library

Alaskans deemed insane/mentally ill often were made to travel through bitter cold weather to get to a port where a ship would take them south on their journey to Morningside Hospital in Portland, Oregon.

UNIT 2: FIRST FIVE YEARS OF STATEHOOD

UNIT TEST

Choose *two* of the following questions to answer in paragraph form. Use as much detail as possible to completely answer the question.

1) Summarize the Saturday Evening Post article titled, "Alaska: Can it survive as a state?" What were some of the rebuttals to the article?

2) Why was the Alaska Marine Highway system important to many Southeastern Alaskans? Why did some call the idea of a ferry system "Downing's Folly"? What did Governor Egan say about the Marine Highway?

3) Describe how mental illness was treated in the early 1900s. How did the Alaska Mental Health Enabling Act change the mental healthcare system?

TEACHER NOTES ABOUT THIS UNIT

UNIT 3: EARTHQUAKE!

LESSON 8: GOOD FRIDAY 1964

FACTS TO KNOW

  Good Friday Earthquake – Historical earthquake on March 27, 1964, that hit Alaska
  Richter Scale/Moment Magnitude Scale – Scales used to measure the intensity of an earthquake
  Tsunamis – Destructive surges of water caused by earthquakes
  Epicenter – The part of the earth's surface that is directly above the place where an earthquake starts

COMPREHENSION QUESTIONS

1) On March _27, 1964_, the _second_-largest earthquake in recorded history struck Alaska. It measured 8.4 on the _Richter Scale_ – experts later upgraded it to 9.2 on the _Moment Magnitude Scale_ as the _Richter Scale_ was determined to be inaccurate at measuring earthquakes above 8.0.

2) Where was the earthquake's epicenter? Where were the effects of the earthquake felt?
The temblor's epicenter was about 75 miles southeast of Anchorage, 54 miles west of Valdez and 15 miles beneath the tranquil waters of Prince William Sound. The effects were felt around the world. (Page 87)

3) Where did the name "tsunami" come from?
Tsunami, an adapted Japanese word meaning "port wave," refers to the fact that the wave's danger and destructive power only becomes evident as it approaches the shore. (Page 88)

4) Describe some of the damage caused by the Good Friday Earthquake.
Entire towns across Southcentral Alaska crumbled, streets buckled and cars, stores and homes dropped into wide crevices that split across the ground. This earthquake altered more of the earth's crust than any other earthquake on record, according to U.S. Geological Survey reports. (Pages 88-89)

5) What was the death toll from the earthquake? Why did experts state that the death toll was remarkably low?
114 people in Alaska, 12 people in California and 4 children in Oregon died as a result of the Alaska earthquake. The immense quake and resulting tsunamis caused massive property damage, but the death toll was remarkably low. Experts say the low death toll can be attributed to a few things: the low population density of the state; few tall buildings in the towns; the time of day the quake occurred; and it hit on a holiday when most Alaskans were home. (Pages 87-89)

6) What did Aunt Phil write in her diary after the earthquake hit?
"Just heard Valdez is gone," wrote Phyllis Downing Carlson in her diary after hearing a ham radio operator sharing the news. She learned that tidal waves had inundated Kodiak, fissures and landslides covered Anchorage and no one had yet heard from other communities along Alaska's coast. She also heard several operators saying prayers for the missing and their families. (Pages 90-91)

DISCUSSION QUESTION

(Discuss this question with your teacher or write your answer in essay form below. Use additional paper if necessary.)

Does your family have a safety plan in the event of an earthquake? (If not, ask your parent or guardian about creating one.) What do you think should be included in your household's plan? What supplies should your family have stored in case of emergency?

ENRICHMENT ACTIVITY

Do you know what to do if an earthquake hits in your area? Create an earthquake safety poster that outlines what people should do in the event of an earthquake. Visit the link below for tips on earthquake safety.

http://www.weatherwizkids.com/weather-safety-earthquake.htm

LEARN MORE

Look for these books at your local library:
Earthquakes, A Primer. Bruce A. Bolt. San Francisco: W.H. Freeman and Company, 1978.

The Day Trees Bent to the Ground: Stories from the '64 Alaska Earthquake, Janet Boyland (Compiler) and Dolores Roguszka (Editor). Publication Consultants, 2005

FIELD TRIP OPPORTUNITIES

If you live in or near Anchorage, make a field trip to:

1) Earthquake Park – This historical park was dedicated to those that lost their lives in the 1964 earthquake and is the only place where you can see the devastation left by the earthquake.

Located at: 5101 Point Woronof Rd, Anchorage AK 99502
http://anchorageparkfoundation.org/directory/earthquake-park/

2) Alaska Experience Theater - You can watch a black and white movie of the 1964 earthquake and the chairs and floor actually shake you as you watch the action.
Located at: 333 W. 4th Ave Anchorage, AK 99501

http://www.alaska.org/detail/alaska-experience-theatre

UNIT 3: EARTHQUAKE!

LESSON 9: ANCHORAGE HIT HARD

FACTS TO KNOW

Genie Chance – Radio and television newscaster who interviewed dozens of Alaskans who survived the Good Friday Earthquake

Robert Atwood – Editor and publisher of *Anchorage Daily Times*

COMPREHENSION QUESTIONS

1) Summarize Robert Atwood's account of the Good Friday Earthquake to Genie Chance.
The veteran newspaperman had just picked up his new trumpet to begin practicing in the living room of his spacious log home when the house began to rock. He quickly realized the house would not stand long with the quake shaking it violently at different angles, so he stumbled out the front door. When he reached his driveway, he turned just in time to see his house destroyed. Atwood said the earth beneath the home twisted the two ends of his house in opposite directions, which seemed to lengthen and then shrink it. (Pages 95-96)

2) How did Robert Atwood describe the sound of the earthquake?
"The noise was terrific," he said. "Just the noise of a dying house ... the glass breaking, the timbers giving, snapping, cracking, splitting – everything tearing apart. ..." (Page 96)

3) Why did Chris von Imhof jump out of a window during the earthquake? What did he compare the earthquake to?
Chris von Imhof was sitting in his second-floor office in the Anchorage International Airport terminal building when the earth began to move. When he tried to go out to the ramp, he found the doors locked because workers were rebuilding the airport. So he had no choice but to jump out of the window. He first slammed his foot through the glass and then leapt out onto the pavement below. He compared it to warfare, as he had lived in Europe during World War II. "The effects are the same, whether it's a bomb blast or an earthquake," he told Chance. (Pages 99-100)

4) Describe some of the damage that Anchorage suffered from the earthquake.
The earthquake caused massive damage to downtown Anchorage, including leveling an apartment building and two parking garages; caused an elementary school and several homes to slide into Ship Creek Valley and settle on top of an Alaska Railroad warehouse; and dropped businesses on three blocks of Fourth Avenue 10 to 20 feet into the ground, according to a U.S. Army Corps of Engineers report. Nine people died in Anchorage that

afternoon: three in the Turnagain-By-The-Sea subdivision, five crushed in the downtown area, and one as the control tower at the airport collapsed. (Page 106)

5) Where did survivors gather after the earthquake?
Survivors huddled in neighbors' homes, community centers like the YMCA, churches and makeshift shelters. They settled in for a night without power, heat or communications. (Page 106)

6) What were some of the critical issues that the city of Anchorage faced after the earthquake?
One of the first critical issues they faced was repairing communications. Military personnel also addressed the need for potable water. Right after the quake, people had to melt snow for drinking water, washing and flushing toilets. The military helped feed the masses, as well, since homes had been destroyed and utilities disrupted. (Pages 108-110)

DISCUSSION QUESTION

(Discuss this question with your teacher or write your answer in essay form below. Use additional paper if necessary.)

What award did Anchorage receive for how it recovered and rebuilt after the Good Friday Earthquake?

_____
_____
_____
_____
_____
_____
_____
_____
_____

ENRICHMENT ACTIVITY

Watch this video to see actual footage of the damage caused by the Good Friday Earthquake: https://www.usgs.gov/media/videos/magnitude-92-1964-great-alaska-earthquake

LEARN MORE

Read more about the Good Friday Earthquake by visiting https://earthquake.usgs.gov/earthquakes/events/alaska1964/

UNIT 3: EARTHQUAKE!

LESSON 10: WILD WAVES BASH WHITTIER
LESSON 11: SEAWATER SEEPS INTO PORTAGE

Note: Read both chapters 10 and 11 before completing this lesson.

FACTS TO KNOW

Whittier – Deep-water port that lies at the western end of the Passage Canal
Portage – Area about 47 miles south of Anchorage in the Turnagain Arm

COMPREHENSION QUESTIONS

1) How did Jerry Wade describe the Good Friday Earthquake to Genie Chance? What happened to his family during the earthquake?
Alaska Railroad employee Jerry Wade told interviewer Genie Chance that he was standing near his trailer home on a bluff 15 feet above the beach in Whittier. When the violent shaking stopped, he watched as water "rushed out of the inlet as through a mighty funnel." Then a wave, which he estimated to be about 20 feet high, rushed onto the beach and swept him, his wife and baby daughter, their trailer home and a railroad flatcar about 400 feet up the beach. His daughter died. (Page 113)

2) How did the earthquake effect the town of Whittier?
The earthquake and giant waves destroyed all communications out of Whittier and cut the spur connecting the town to the Alaska Railroad line out to Portage. A U.S. Coast Guard plane flew over Whittier the next morning and those on board saw oil tanks burning. Just after noon, a Pacific Northern Airlines pilot reported Whittier was "all aflame" as he passed overhead. The port was not as badly damaged as initially thought, however. The power plant remained in operation and major port buildings suffered little damage. (Pages 113-114)

3) The city of Whittier, *incorporated* in 1969, grew to around *300* people who now call it home. The town became known for *commercial fishing, recreation and tourism*.

4) How long did the earthquake last in the Portage area? Why did it last this long?
The earthquake lasted 18 minutes in Portage due to the area's thick underlying beds of clay, according to Alaska Railroad records. (Page 117)

5) What prevented the residents of the Portage area from evacuating?
The residents of Portage had not been able to evacuate due to the destruction of highway bridges and landslides on both sides of the area. The military sent helicopters to rescue residents. (Pages 120-121)

6) How long did it take the U.S. Army to reach Portage? Why did the military have to return to Portage a few weeks later?

The U.S. Army finally reached Portage on Tuesday afternoon, four days after the earthquake, and they had fought the highway around the clock to get there. Then when high spring tides flooded their village and carried giant chunks of ice through their already battered community, they sent out an urgent call for rescue. Two military helicopters responded to evacuate 12 people – 10 went to Girdwood and two to Elmendorf Air Force Base in Anchorage. An Army chopper carried another eight people to the high school at Girdwood. (Pages 122-124)

DISCUSSION QUESTION

(Discuss this question with your teacher or write your answer in essay form below. Use additional paper if necessary.)

What are some ways that we can help others during a natural disaster like an earthquake or a hurricane?

___

ENRICHMENT ACTIVITY

Do you have a relative who remembers the Good Friday Earthquake of 1964? If so, ask them what they remember about that day. Come up with at least three questions to ask before your interview.

LEARN MORE

Read more about tsunamis by visiting http://www.nationalgeographic.com/environment/natural-disasters/tsunamis/

UNIT 3: EARTHQUAKE!

LESSON 12: ALASKA RAILROAD DAMAGED
LESSON 13: SEWARD BURNS
LESSON 14: VALDEZ WASHED AWAY

Note: Read chapters 12, 13 and 14 before completing this lesson.

FACTS TO KNOW

Alaska Railroad – Railroad that provides rail transportation from Seward to Alaska's interior town of Fairbanks

Seward – Town located on Ressurection Bay, about 125 miles south of Anchorage via train or New Seward Highway

Valdez - Town located on Prince William Sound, about 300 miles from Anchorage via Parks and Richardson highways

COMPREHENSION QUESTIONS

Summarize how the Good Friday Earthquake effected the following places. Describe one eyewitness account for each location.

1) Alaska Railroad: *(Answers will vary. See Pages 126-129)*

2) Seward: *(Answers will vary. See Pages 130-140)*

49

3) Valdez: *(Answers will vary. See Pages 141-151)*

4) What are some similarities you noticed between the eyewitness accounts in Chapters 12-14? *(Answers will vary)*

ENRICHMENT ACTIVITY

You have read several eyewitness accounts of the Good Friday Earthquake. For the remainder of Unit 3, you will be working on your own short story that takes place during the March 1964 earthquake. Take some time during this lesson to create an outline for your story. Who are your characters? In which city will your story take place? What events will you write about?

LEARN MORE

Read more about the Good Friday Earthquake by visiting https://www.ncei.noaa.gov/news/great-alaska-earthquake

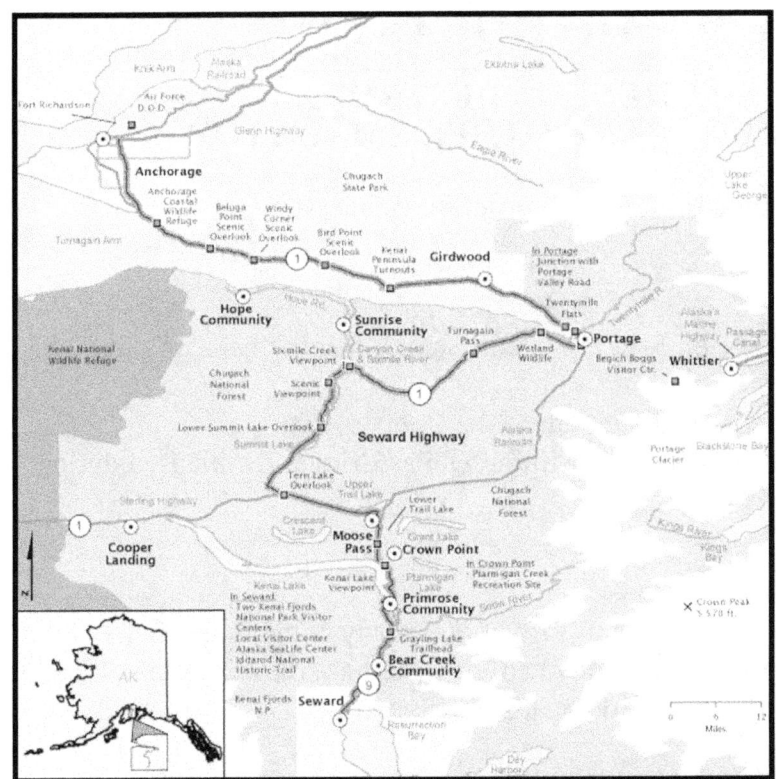

Left: This map shows the 125-mile route from Anchorage to Seward along the New Seward Highway. This is basically the same route the Alaska Railroad takes, too.

Bottom: This map shows the almost 300-mile route from Anchorage to Valdez, which goes along the Parks Highway to Palmer and then changes to the Richardson Highway.

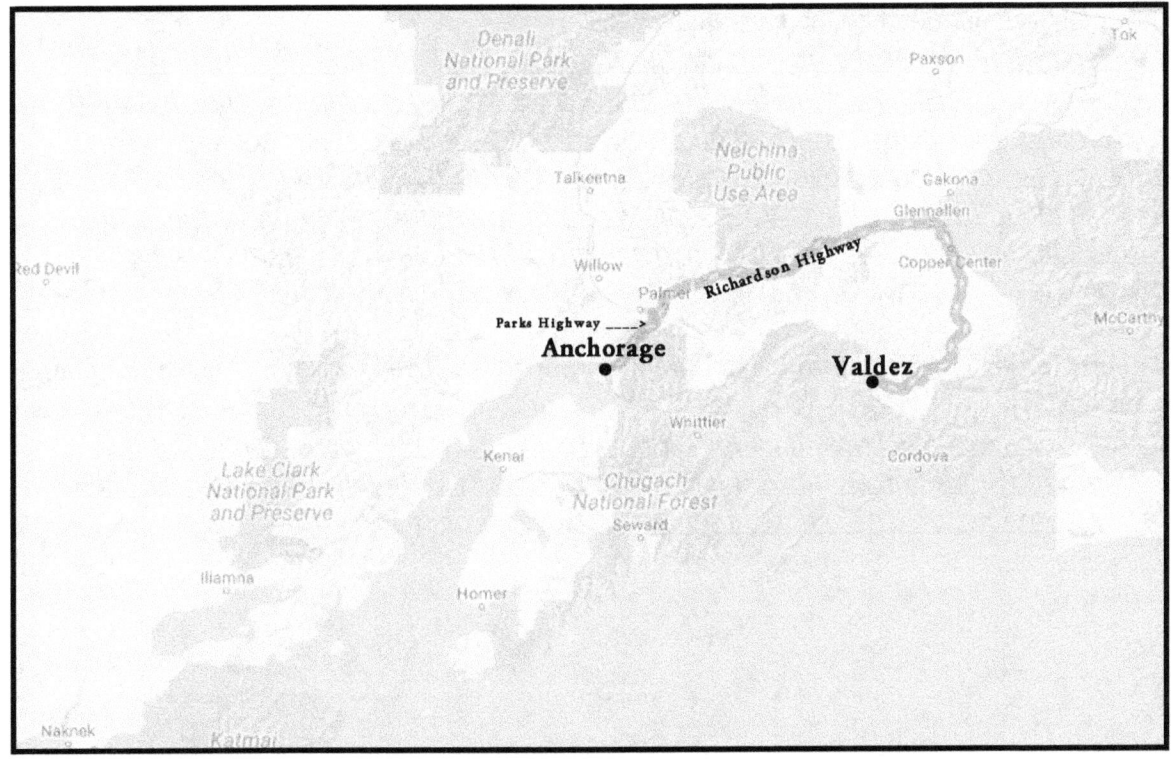

UNIT 3: EARTHQUAKE!

LESSON 15: CHENEGA DESTROYED
LESSON 16: CORDOVA AND OTHER SMALL TOWNS

Note: Read both chapters 15 and 16 before completing this lesson.

FACTS TO KNOW

Chenega – Oldest Native village on Prince William Sound; means "beneath the mountain"

Cordova – Small town located near the mouth of the Copper River

Miles Glacier Bridge – Also known as the Million Dollar Bridge; it collapsed during the 1964 earthquake

COMPREHENSION QUESTIONS

1) _Chenega_ suffered the highest percentage of loss of _life_ of any community in the Good Friday Earthquake. The three giant _waves_ generated from the massive earthquake killed _23_ villagers, more than one-third of the settlement's population.

2) How long had the Chenega people lived on their land before the earthquake? What did the survivors do after the earthquake?
Chenega people had lived, fished and harvested the land for more than 10,000 years. Survivors, who spent the night huddled in the snow around a campfire high on a hill overlooking their ruined village, had no choice but to move away from their beloved village. They chose to resettle on a hillside above Crab Bay on Evans Island, about 20 miles south of the old village. After a few years of negotiations with the government, Chenegans began building their new community in 1984 and named it Chenega Bay. (Pages 153-155)

3) Did Cordova experience a lot of damage compared to other cities in Alaska? Explain your answer.
Cordova suffered much less damage than its sister cities. With the exception of the collapse of the Million Dollar Bridge and some houses and boats that were washed out by the shoreline, the city suffered minimal damage. (Pages 156-159)

4) Briefly summarize how each of the following towns was affected by the 1964 earthquake:

Homer: *(Answers will vary. See Page 160)*

Seldovia: *(Answers will vary. See Page 161)*

Kenai-Soldotna: *(Answers will vary. See Page 162)*

DISCUSSION QUESTION

(Discuss this question with your teacher or write your answer in essay form below. Use additional paper if necessary.)

In what ways do you think the Good Friday Earthquake changed the history of Alaska?

_____
_____
_____
_____
_____
_____
_____
_____
_____
_____
_____
_____
_____

ENRICHMENT ACTIVITY

Continue working on your story that takes place during the March 1964 Good Friday Earthquake. Take some time during this lesson to finish developing your characters and setting and then begin writing your story. Focus writing a strong beginning that will draw your readers into your story.

LEARN MORE

See more pictures from the Good Friday Earthquake in Alaska by visiting https://www.thealaskalife.com/blog/1964-earthquake-photo-gallery/

Tidal waves can cause massive damage to coastal communities – this photo shows St. Michael in 1913 when a tidal wave unexectedly hit its shores.

UNIT 3: EARTHQUAKE!

LESSON 17: TIDAL WAVES OVERTAKE KODIAK
LESSON 18: VILLAGES NEAR KODIAK IN RUINS

Note: Read both chapters 17 and 18 before completing this lesson.

FACTS TO KNOW

Tidal wave – Unusually high sea wave caused by an earthquake
Kodiak – Main city on Kodiak Island that experienced strong tidal waves from the 1964 earthquake

COMPREHENSION QUESTIONS

1) How did eyewitnesses in Kodiak describe the Good Friday Earthquake?
Eyewitnesses said they heard a rumbling sound five seconds before feeling the first tremor. At 5:36 p.m. on March 27, 1964, the ground slowly began to shake. Within a minute of the initial tremor, the shaking grew more intense. (Page 164)

2) What was the radio report about Kodiak on the day of the earthquake?
Kodiak residents heard an announcement come over a shortwave radio that Kodiak was sinking into the sea. (Page 167)

3) How much destruction did tidal waves cause to Kodiak?
The tidal waves killed 14 and caused around $24 million in damage. They destroyed more than 100 homes, as well as the telephone utility, movie theater, grocery store, dry goods store, bars, fish canneries, boats and docks. (Page 169)

4) Briefly summarize what happened to the following villages near Kodiak during the earthquake:

Afognak: *(Answers will vary. See Pages 172-175)* _____

Old Harbor: *(Answers will vary. See Pages 175-177)*

Ouzinkie: *(Answers will vary. See Pages 177-179)*

Kaguyak: *(Answers will vary. See Pages 180-182)*

ENRICHMENT ACTIVITY

You have read several eyewitness accounts of the Good Friday Earthquake and are creating your own short story that takes place during the March 1964 earthquake. Continue developing your characters, place and plot of this story during the rest of Unit 3. Take some time during this lesson to begin writing the conclusion of your story.

LEARN MORE

Read about why Alaska has so many earthquakes by visiting https://earthquake.alaska.edu/earthquakes/about

Courtesy National Guard

Several tidal waves bashed Kodiak on March 27, 1964. They destroyed buildings and tossed boats into the center of town, as seen in this photograph.

MAP ACTIVITY

Locate the following places on the map below:

1) Kodiak 2) Seward 3) Valdez 4) Cordova 5) Chenega Bay 6) Whittier
7) Seldovia 8) Homer 9) Old Harbor 10) Ouzinkie 11) Anchorage

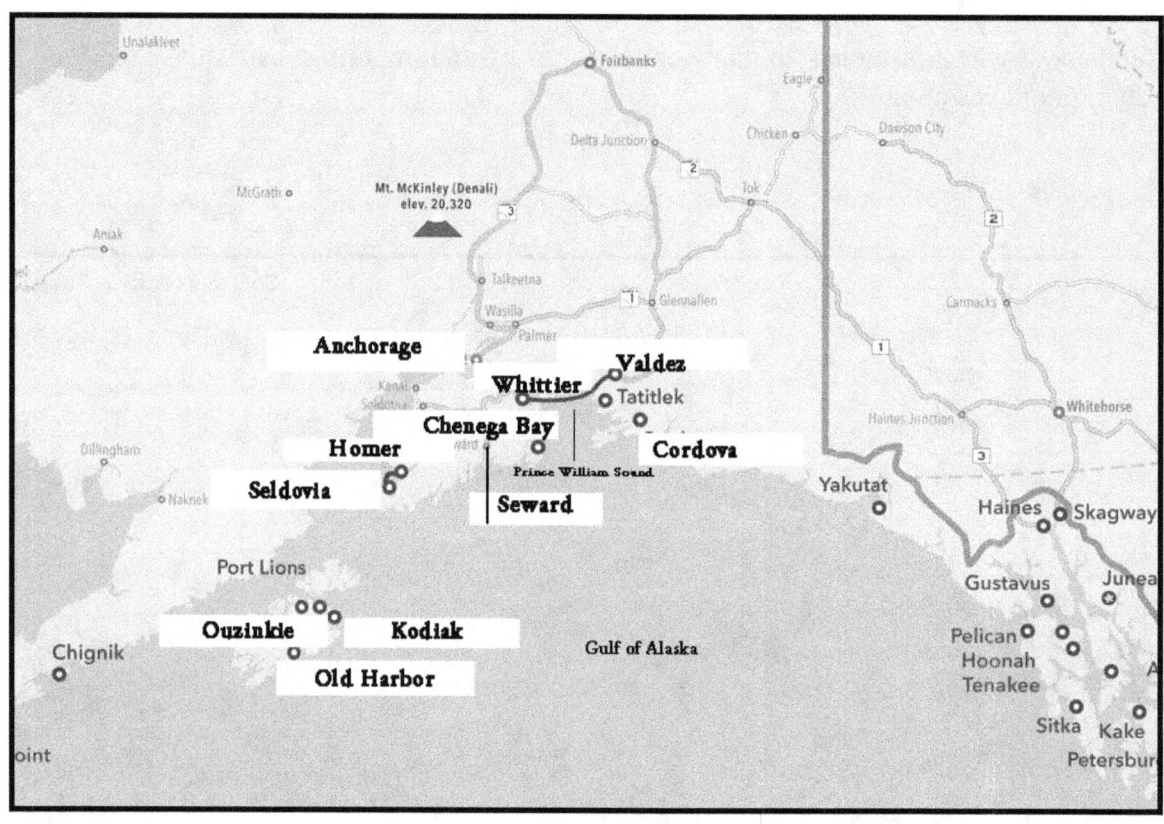

UNIT 3: EARTHQUAKE!

LESSON 19: ALASKANS LEARN THEY'RE NOT ALONE
LESSON 20: REBUILDING BETTER THAN BEFORE

Note: Read both chapters 19 and 20 before completing this lesson.

FACTS TO KNOW

The Salvation Army – A Christian organization that is one of the world's largest providers of social aid

American Red Cross – A humanitarian organization that provides emergency assistance and disaster relief

All-American City Award – Award given by the National Civic League annually to recognize 10 cities whose citizens work together to identify and tackle community-wide challenges and achieve uncommon results

Federal Disaster Relief – Federal funds used to pay for ongoing recovery projects from disasters

Government bonds – A bond is an IOU of the United States Treasury and is considered the safest security in the investment world

COMPREHENSION QUESTIONS

1) What was the overwhelming emotion that many Alaskans experienced after the Good Friday Earthquake? Who was one of the first people who shared a message with Alaskans? How did that help?
In those first hours after the devastating earthquake and tidal waves of Good Friday 1964, the overwhelming emotion for many Alaskans was one of isolation. One of the first messages heard came from Britain's Queen Elizabeth, who had expressed her sympathy to U.S. President Lyndon B. Johnson. Many Alaskans did not feel so alone anymore. They knew the world cared about them just as they cared about each other. (Page 183)

2) What were some of the ways that Alaskans helped those hit hardest by the earthquake?
Around 200 laborers, 30 carpenters, 31 carpenter helpers, 32 heavy equipment operators and 32 truck drivers from Kotzebue, Point Hope, Kivalina, Kiana, Shungnak, Noorvik, Noatak, Selawik and Buckland offered to help rebuild the stricken areas. Barrow, the nation's most northern community, quickly began raising a disaster fund. And from undamaged Juneau, Ketchikan and other Southeast communities came an overwhelming flood of concern and offers of assistance. (Page 184)

3) How did Americans in the Lower 48 help the survivors of Alaska's earthquake?
Americans everywhere moved rapidly to help their northern brothers and sisters. The Salvation Army kept a steady flow of supplies on the way to displaced families. And using Seattle as its base, the American Red Cross immediately organized their facilities. (Page 185)

4) Alaska's Good Friday Earthquake was ranked No. 4 on the list of major news stories for the year *1964* in a poll conducted by *The Associated Press* of the nation's news editors. It was beat out of first place by the campaign and landslide election of U.S. President *Lyndon B. Johnson*; the ouster of *Russia*'s Nikita Khrushchev, which ranked No. 2; and the continuing *civil rights* struggle that came in No. 3.

5) How did Alaska's earthquake alter Alaska's outlook for the future? Explain your answer.
The massive tremors that hit the Southcentral coastline altered the entire outlook of the nation's newest state – the devastation set loose a new spirit in a state already overflowing with hope and plans. Alaskans immediately rolled up their sleeves and began rebuilding their communities. Undaunted by the incredible destruction and the enormous job ahead, Alaskans looked to the future as they had in the past with their faith in Alaska.

Historians agree that although the 1964 earthquake brought Alaskans to their knees, it actually helped the state's economy by flooding federal dollars north for recovery. Page 195)

Alaska also saw a spike in its population. It grew at a rate well above the national average – 14.4 percent compared to 8.1 percent – and had the fifth-highest state growth rate in the United States, according to the U.S. Department of Commerce. Alaska's future looked bright. (Page 198)

DISCUSSION QUESTION

(Discuss this question with your teacher or write your answer in essay form below. Use additional paper if necessary.)

Do you think that the earthquake unified Alaskans? Explain your answer.

_____
_____
_____
_____
_____
_____
_____

ENRICHMENT ACTIVITY

You have read several eyewitness accounts of the Good Friday Earthquake and are creating your own short story that takes place during the March 1964 earthquake. Take some time during this lesson to write the final draft of your story. Read your story aloud to check for mistakes and/or find areas where you can improve it. Then share your story with your teacher/class.

TIME TO REVIEW

Review Chapters 8-20 of your book before moving on to the Unit Review. See how many questions you can answer without looking at your book.

U.S. military troops immediately went into action to help earthquake victims in Anchorage. The U.S. Army Signal Corps captured this photo of the 521st Transportation Company serving hot food late into the evening following the massive quake.

Earthquake!
Crossword Puzzle

Read Across and Down clues and fill in blank boxes that match numbers on the clues

Across
3 Lack of light
5 Scattered fragments of things destroyed
7 This oldest Native village on Prince William Sound was wiped out by tidal waves
8 Break or cause to break without a complete separation of the parts
11 Great destruction
15 The point on the earth's surface vertically above the focus of an earthquake
18 Wiped out
20 Place where ships load or unload
21 These were damaged so badly that trains could not run until repaired
22 People with this type of radio transmitted messages across Alaska
25 Live through a dangerous event
26 The mainland and spit of this town dropped 2 to 6 feet
28 This city, on an island of the same name, was severely damaged by tidal waves
29 Japanese word for "port wave"
31 Day that the Great Alaska Earthquake struck in 1964
32 Save someone from danger
33 1964 Alaska earthquake measured 9.2 on this scale
37 Some people said the beginning of the 1964 earthquake sounded like this
43 Thick underlying beds of clay made the earthquake in this area last 18 minutes
45 The sliding down of a mass of earth
46 One side of Fourth Avenue in this city dropped 10 to 20 feet
47 Name of WWII pre-fabricated portable truss bridge put across creeks to connect Kenai Peninsula with road system
49 Move someone from a place of danger to a safe place
50 Exceptionally large
52 1964 Alaska earthquake measured 8.4 on this scale
54 The Elmendorf bakery made 14,000 pounds of this every day for four days

---

Down
1 One gets this when fuel is ignited
2 This town at the western end of Passage Canal was devastated by giant waves
4 A state of stunned confusion; dazed
6 This town on Resurrection Bay burned when oil tanks split and exploded
9 This country had the largest earthquake ever recorded at 9.5 in 1960
10 Area along which a large body of water meets the land
12 Smaller earthquakes following the main shock of a large earthquake
13 Another word for extreme fear
14 An instrument that measures and records details of earthquakes
16 A platform extending from a shore over water where boats may tie up
17 The Million Dollar Bridge near this town collapsed
19 These systems of spreading news were severely damaged
23 A sudden slip along a fault between a subducting and an overriding plate
24 A long, narrow opening of the earth
25 People had to melt this for drinking water
27 Beautiful homes in this Anchorage subdivision split and fell as a bluff broke into pieces
30 Alaska's 1964 quake released more energy than 10 million of these
34 Editor and publisher of the *Anchorage Daily Times*
35 Unable to leave because of a problem
36 Military rescue workers had to bulldoze through several of these on the New Seward Highway to get to the Portage area

Earthquake!
Crossword Puzzle Key

Down (Continued)

38 Physical harm to something that makes it useless
39 People stacked these in an effort to prevent flooding near Girdwood
40 A sudden event, such as an earthquake, that causes great damage or loss of life
41 This community near Portage ended up below sea level after the earth shifted and had to move
42 Another word for earthquake
44 Contaminated with harmful substances
48 Water needed to have this done in order to be safe to drink
51 Tidal waves destroyed this town situated on Prince William Sound
53 This branch of the U.S. military fed Anchorage residents for several days

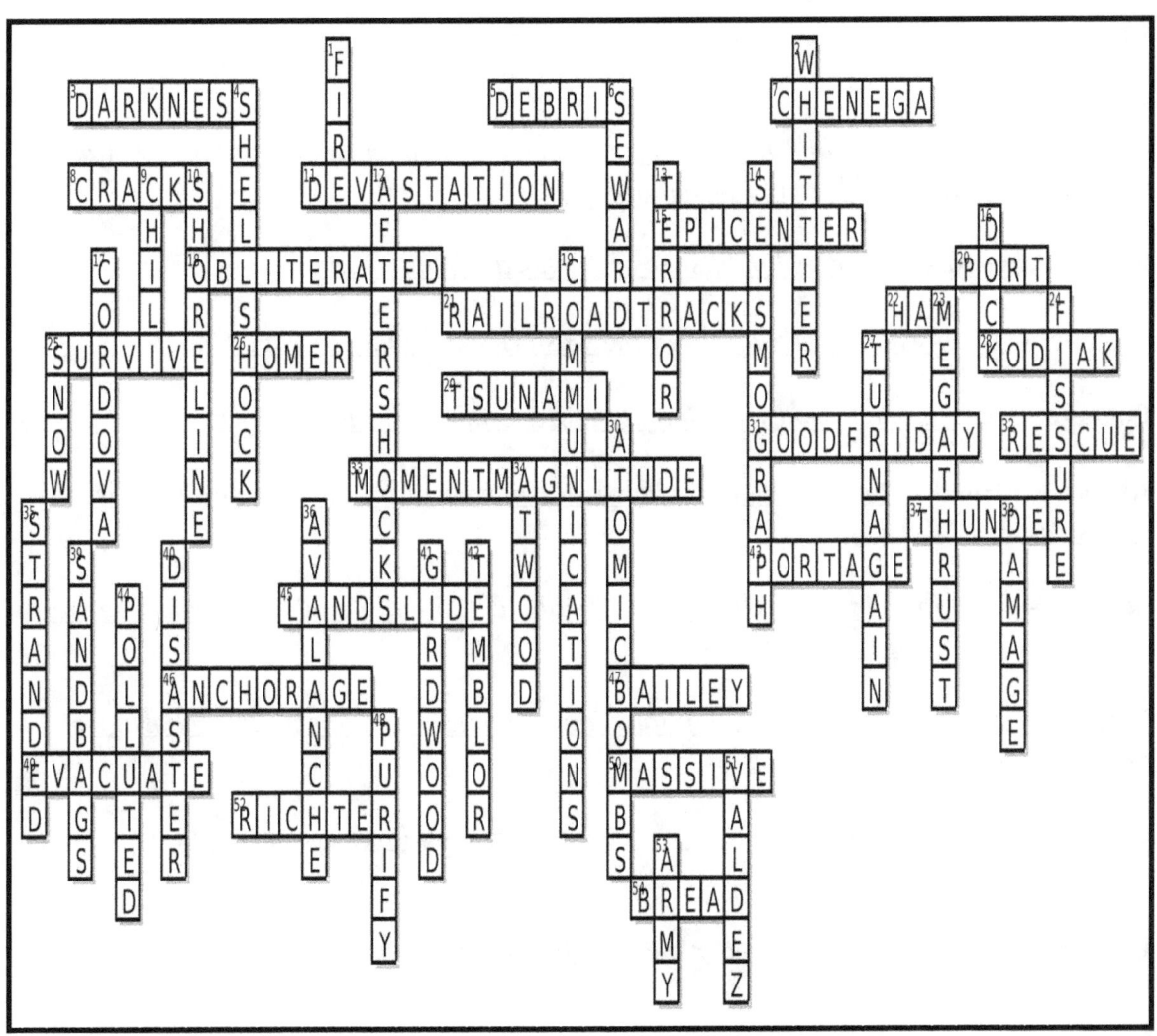

63

UNIT 3: EARTHQUAKE!

REVIEW LESSONS 8-20

Write down what you remember about:

Good Friday Earthquake – <u>Historical earthquake in 1964 that hit Alaska</u>

Richter Scale/Moment Magnitude Scale – <u>Scales used to measure the intensity of an earthquake</u>

Tsunamis – <u>Destructive surges of water caused by earthquakes</u>

Epicenter – <u>The part of the earth's surface that is directly above the place where an earthquake starts</u>

Genie Chance – <u>Radio and television newscaster who interviewed dozens of Alaskans who survived the Good Friday Earthquake</u>

Robert Atwood – <u>Editor and publisher of Anchorage Daily Times</u>

Whittier – <u>Deep-water port that lies at the western end of the Passage Canal</u>

Portage – <u>Area about 47 miles south of Anchorage in the Turnagain Arm</u>

Alaska Railroad – <u>Railroad that provides rail transportation from Seward to Alaska's interior town of Fairbanks</u>

Seward – <u>Town located on Ressurection Bay, about 125 miles south of Anchorage via train or New Seward Highway</u>

Valdez – <u>Town located on Prince William Sound, about 300 miles from Anchorage via Parks and Richardson highways</u>

Chenega – <u>Oldest Native village on Prince William Sound; means "beneath the mountain"</u>

Cordova – <u>Small town located near the mouth of the Copper River</u>

Miles Glacier Bridge – *Also known as the Million Dollar Bridge; it collapsed during the 1964 earthquake*

Tidal wave – *Unusually high sea wave caused by an earthquake*

Kodiak – *Main city on Kodiak Island that experienced strong tidal waves from the 1964 earthquake*

The Salvation Army – *A Christian organization that is one of the world's largest providers of social aid*

American Red Cross – *A humanitarian organization that provides emergency assistance and disaster relief*

All-American City Award – *Award given by the National Civic League annually to recognize 10 cities whose citizens work together to identify and tackle community-wide challenges and achieve uncommon results*

Federal Disaster Relief – *Federal funds used to pay for ongoing recovery projects from disasters*

Government bonds – *A bond is an IOU of the United States Treasury and is considered the safest security in the investment world*

Fill in the blanks:

1) The *second*-largest earthquake in recorded history struck on *March 27, 1964*. It measured 8.4 on the *Richter* Scale – experts later upgraded it to 9.2 on the *Moment Magnitude* Scale as the *Richter* Scale was determined to be inaccurate at measuring earthquakes above 8.0.

2) The temblor's *epicenter* was about 75 miles southeast of Anchorage, 54 miles west of Valdez and 15 miles beneath the tranquil waters of *Prince William Sound*.

3) *Tsunami*, an adapted *Japanese* word meaning "port wave," refers to the fact that the wave's danger and destructive power only becomes evident as it approaches the *shore*.

4) Radio and television newscaster *Genie Chance* interviewed dozens of people across Alaska who survived the *Good Friday* Earthquake on March 27, 1964. She then compiled the interviews and published a document in 1966 titled *"Chronology of Physical Events of the Alaskan Earthquake."*

5) The great earthquake of March 27, 1964, destroyed the *air traffic control tower* at Anchorage International Airport, killing one *traffic controller* on duty that day.

6) In 1965, the National Civic League awarded *Anchorage* with the coveted *All-American City* award – along with Seward and Valdez – for how it *recovered and rebuilt* following the Good Friday earthquake.

7) The residents of Portage had not been able to *evacuate* due to the destruction of *roads and bridges* and landslides on both sides of town. They spent a fearful night with mighty *aftershocks* hitting often, and they worried about *tidal* waves.

8) *Oil tanks* near the docks in *Seward* exploded and burned during the 1964 Good Friday Earthquake. *Tidal waves* from various sources created havoc on the small town, including an underwater landslide beneath the waterfront; the sloshing effect in *Resurrection* Bay; and displacement water from the earthquake fracturing the floor beneath *Prince William* Sound.

9) Alaska Gov. *William A. Egan,* one of *Valdez*'s most famous residents, arrived with other state officials to survey the damage on Sunday afternoon. As their plane approached the airport, they saw tons of *debris* floating on an oil-covered bay. A *house* drifted a half-mile offshore. Overturned *boats* and *dead fish* were everywhere, according to a newspaper story of the governor's visit.

10) *Chenega*, the oldest *Native village* on Prince William Sound, was destroyed during the earthquake. The *tidal waves* wiped out the oldest continuously inhabited *Native* community in the area – a place where the *Chenega* people had lived, fished and harvested the land for more than *10,000* years.

11) *Cordova* did not suffer as much from the great quake or tsunamis as its sister cities. It did see damage to its *waterfront*, and the nearby *Million Dollar* Bridge collapsed.

12) The U.S. military brought in a *Baily* bridge, commonly used during World War II, to connect the people of the *Kenai* Peninsula to the rest of Alaska.

13) *Tidal waves* killed 14 and caused around *$24 million* in damage to the island town of Kodiak. They destroyed more than *100* homes, as well as *the telephone utility, movie theater, grocery store, dry goods store, bars, fish canneries, boats and docks*.

14) Tsunamis destroyed the village at *Afognak*. The villagers didn't think it feasible to rebuild at the same location so they rebuilt their community on Kizhuyak Bay on *Kodiak* Island and renamed it *Port Lions*.

15) Old Harbor, on the southeast coast of *Kodiak Island*, suffered subtantial damage but its residents decided to *rebuild* in the same location.

16) Tidal waves inundated *Ouzinkie*, on the west side of Spruce Island, about 12 miles north of the city of *Kodiak*. The village existed for the *fishing industry* and most villagers lost their livlihood when a big piece of the *cannery* was washed out to sea.

17) In those first hours after the devastating earthquake and tidal waves of Good Friday 1964, the overwhelming emotion for many Alaskans was one of *isolation*. In most of the stricken towns, *local radio* and *television stations* dropped off the air when electricity went out. Alaskans felt *alone and cut off*.

18) Alaskans learned there were no *rich* or *poor*. The earthquake not only leveled buildings, it also leveled distinctions, *political* as well as *financial* and *social*. Politicians forgot their differences and all Alaskans were *united* in their misfortune.

19) With well wishes from so many people all around the world, and *financial* assistance from the federal *government*, Alaskans did, indeed, get back to business. The motto across Alaska became, "*Better than before*."

UNIT 3: EARTHQUAKE!

UNIT TEST

Choose *three* of the following questions to answer in paragraph form. Use as much detail as possible to completely answer the question.

1) What Alaska cities were most devastated by the Good Friday Earthquake? What aid was sent to the cities? How did they rebuild?

2) Summarize at least three eyewitness accounts that were covered in the unit.

3) How did the earthquake effect Alaska's economy?

4) What emotion did many Alaskan's feel after the earthquake? Why? What events helped Alaskans to unify after the earthquake?

TEACHER NOTES ABOUT THIS UNIT

TEACHER NOTES ABOUT THIS UNIT

UNIT 4: ALASKA LAND IN DISPUTE

LESSON 21: HOMESTEADERS HEAD NORTH

FACTS TO KNOW

59ers – Adventurers from Michigan who traveled to Alaska to seek a better life in 1959
Homestead – A piece of public land given to settlers for cultivation
President Abraham Lincoln – Sixteenth president of the United States who signed the Homestead Act in 1862

COMPREHENSION QUESTIONS

1) Who were the 59ers? Why did they travel to Alaska? How did they travel there?
The 59ers were people from Detroit who traveled by caravan, consisting of 17 cars, six camper-trailers and a 1936 moving van named "The Monstrosity." The group left Michigan and headed north on March 5, 1959. Most of these adventurers had blue-collar jobs and hoped the grass might be greener in the Last Frontier. The group included brick-layers, carpenters, mechanics and other tradesmen who felt they had no future in Detroit with its stagnant economy and double-digit unemployment numbers. They thought Alaska held more promise. (Page 199)

2) How long did it take the 59ers to reach Alaska? Did all the families make it to Alaska? Explain your answer.
It took the group 10 days to reach Alaska. The journey proved too much for nine families. They dropped out before reaching the border and returned to Michigan. (Page 202)

3) Were the 59ers welcomed by Alaskans when they arrived? Explain your answer.
Yes. Enthusiastic well-wishers greeted the bunch and welcomed them to the new state. Then the Alaska State Troopers escorted the caravan from Palmer into Anchorage, where a raucous celebration in their honor exploded along Fourth Avenue. Sgt. Gardner B. White Jr. of Elmendorf Air Force Base entertained them with a song he had written in their honor, titled "My New Alaska Home." (Page 202)

4) What kind of difficulties did the 59ers face in Alaska?
Cultivating land for crops was hard or impossible in the soil found in many areas of the state. Homesteaders faced other hardships, too, including remoteness, severely cold weather, short growing seasons, high cost of supplies, no market for crops and lack of roads. (Page 204)

5) When did homesteading end in Alaska? Why?
Homesteading ended in Alaska on Oct. 21, 1986. Tens of millions of acres of federal land had been withdrawn from homestead entry to allow the state and Native corporations to select land under terms in the 1958 Alaska Statehood Act and the 1971 Alaska Native Claims Settlement Act. (Page 208)

6) Who was the last homesteader in Alaska?
Kenneth Deardorff was the last homesteader in Alaska (and the nation) – he received the patent to his claim in the late 1980s. The Vietnam War veteran from California originally made his way to Alaska looking for work with the U.S. Geological Survey, but once in the Great Land, decided to homestead. (Page 208)

DISCUSSION QUESTION

(Discuss this question with your teacher or write your answer in essay form below. Use additional paper if necessary.)

What are some of the reasons that many wanted to leave the Lower 48 and claim a homestead in Alaska?

_____
_____
_____
_____
_____
_____
_____
_____
_____
_____
_____
_____
_____
_____
_____

ENRICHMENT ACTIVITY

Spend some time exploring the link below to learn more about homesteading in Alaska. Watch the video to learn about what life was like for homesteaders.
https://www.alaskacenters.gov/homestead.cfm

LEARN MORE

Read excerpts from *Alaska Native Land Claims,* a book by Robert D. Arnold, by visiting http://www.alaskool.org/projects/ancsa/landclaims/LandClaimsTOC.htm

UNIT 4: ALASKA LAND IN DISPUTE

LESSON 22: WHO OWNS THE LAND?

FACTS TO KNOW

1884 Organic Act – Provided Alaska its first civilian government and contained language that set the stage for settlement of land claims decades later
Reservations – Lands held in trust for Native people by the government
Land Claim – Petition to own a segment of land

COMPREHENSION QUESTIONS

1) Did Native Alaskans approve of Russia selling Alaska to the United States? Explain your answer.
Many Native Alaskans did not know that Russia sold Alaska to the United States. When Tlingit chiefs learned about the sale, they immediately voiced their opinion that Russia had no right to do so. They also told a U.S. Treasury Department agent that Russians had lived in their country only because the Natives had given them permission to do so. (Pages 211-212)

2) When the U.S. Navy began governing Alaska in 1877, how did it handle disputes between the new settlers and the Chilkat Tlingits?
Following discoveries of gold in the 1880s, many prospectors began arriving in Southeast. At first the Chilkat Tlingits refused to allow travel through their territory to the gold fields, but the Navy convinced them otherwise by sending a warship equipped with a Gatling gun to escort several sailboats carrying armed prospectors into the Chilkat area. (Page 212)

3) What protections did the 1884 Organic Act offer Native Alaskans?
It gave protection to miners' claims and lands used by missionaries – but only a promise of continued use and occupancy of lands to holders of aboriginal rights, according to the Alaska Native Foundation. Historians say the intention of the act, which provided the first civil government for the new possession, was "to save from all possible invasion the rights of Indian residents of Alaska" until such time they could "ascertain what their claims were." (Page 213)

4) What legal step did the Tlingit and Haida people take to gain control of their land in 1935? Did it work? Explain your answer.
They filed suit against the federal government for taking land that belonged to them. In 1935, they asked for $35 million to pay for the land and hunting and fishing rights that had been taken from them by the U.S. Forest Service. That legal battle lasted for the next three

decades, until judges sided with the Natives in the late 1950s. The U.S. Court of Claims early in 1968 awarded the Tlingit and Haida Indians $7.5 million for claims against land. (Pages 214-215)

5) What was the purpose of reservations? Why did many disagree with the idea of reservations?
The Indian Reorganization Act, enacted in 1934, allowed the Department of the Interior to establish reservations in Alaska. This would not mean giving Natives title to land, but instead the department would hold title in trust for them. Non-Natives in Alaska feared this move would lock up lands, and Natives feared they would be confined to small areas with limited resources like the Indians in the Continental United States. Public opinion was that reservations promoted racial segregation. (Page 215)

6) Why did many Native Alaskans believe that statehood would be the key to solving Native land claims issues? Was it?
While it did not solve land claim issues, the act had a disclaimer that said the new state and its people disclaimed all right or title to lands that "may be held by Eskimos, Indians or Aleuts" or held in trust for them. That language set the stage for a land rights battle and settlement of mammoth proportions. That long-delayed lawsuit against the federal government by the Tlingits and Haidas, ruled in the Natives' favor in 1959, bolstered the position that Alaska's First People owned the land. (Pages 216-217)

DISCUSSION QUESTION

(Discuss this question with your teacher or write your answer in essay form below. Use additional paper if necessary.)

Why was it important for Native Alaskans to get title to land?

_____
_____
_____

ENRICHMENT ACTIVITY

Learn more about Alaska Native cultures by visiting http://www.akhistorycourse.org/alaskas-cultures/alaska-native-heritage-center. Explore each link on the Webpage to read about each Native culture. Which group is most interesting to you? Why?

LEARN MORE

Learn more about the history of Native land claim issues by visiting http://www.akhistorycourse.org/governing-alaska/native-citizenship-and-land-issues

UNIT 4: ALASKA LAND IN DISPUTE

LESSON 23: ROCK, NATIVE UNITY AND LAND CLAIMS

FACTS TO KNOW

Howard Rock – Founder of the *Tundra Times* newspaper
Emil Notti – Alaska Native leader and activist who fought for Native land rights
Alaska Federation of Natives – Statewide organization formed to bring together Natives from dozens of villages and tribes to address land claim issues
Alaska Native Claims Settlement Act – Document signed by President Richard Nixon that gave 44 million acres of land and $962.5 million to Alaska Natives

COMPREHENSION QUESTIONS

1) What was "Project Chariot"? Why were Alaska Natives opposed to it?
It was the U.S. government's plan to detonate a nuclear blast and create a harbor in the Arctic for shipping minerals and other goods from northwest Alaska. Alaska Natives were concerned about their land and people near the proposed blast sites. This led researchers to compile "Project Chariot Marine Mammal Study, Cape Thompson, 1960-61," a study of the effects a nuclear blast might have on marine life in the area. (Page 221)

2) What did the Arctic Slope Native Association ask Howard Rock to start? How did this endeavor help Alaska Natives?
The Arctic Slope Native Association asked Rock to start the Tundra Times newspaper. The association saw it as an avenue for Alaska's Native people to be part of their own destiny. The paper changed the way many Natives saw themselves. Along with journalist Tom Snapp, Rock covered issues that affected Alaska's Native people and encouraged them to have pride and respect for their heritage and cultures – and to fight for them. (Page 230)

3) Why did U.S. Secretary of the Interior Stewart Udall issue an injunction in 1966 to stop transfer of title from federal to state ownership? How did this help bring the issue of Native land claims to the forefront?
Alaska Natives began filing protests on a staggering amount of land. Some groups filed on land that other groups filed on. He issued an injunction in 1966 that tied up transfer of title from federal to state ownership until the Native land claims issue was settled. This not only stopped the state from choosing land, it also stalled non-Native homestead applications and disrupted business plans for many companies. Because of this, the state wanted the issue settled quickly. (Pages 232-233)

4) What did Emil Notti and Willie Hensley do in May 1967 to make sure that the Native point of view about Native land claims was heard by the government?
Notti and Democratic State Rep. Willie Hensley, a Kotzebue Eskimo, flew to the nation's capital to join in discussions about Native land claims that originally only included Gov. Hickel, Interior Secretary Udall and other officials, which also may have included President Lyndon B. Johnson. (Pages 234-235)

5) How did the oil industry play a key role in the signing of the Alaska Native Claims Settlement Act?
Oil companies met with leaders of the Alaska Federation of Natives in 1968 in an attempt to sway them into settling with the state and federal governments. Oil companies joined Alaska Natives' calls for settling the land claims issue following a major discovery of crude oil at Prudhoe Bay. (Page 236)

6) What compromise did the Alaska Native Claims Settlement Act provide?
Congress awarded Alaska's aboriginal people 44 million acres of land and $962.5 million – the largest settlement the U.S. government ever had made with Native Americans. In exchange, Alaska's Natives gave up their aboriginal land claims, which ended the land freeze and opened the door for the oil pipeline on the North Slope. They also surrendered their aboriginal hunting and fishing rights. (Pages 236-237)

DISCUSSION QUESTION

(Discuss this question with your teacher or write your answer in essay form below. Use additional paper if necessary.)

How did the Alaska Native Claims Settlement Act change the lives of Alaska Natives?

ENRICHMENT ACTIVITY

There were many steps that happened before the Alaska Native Claims Settlement Act was signed into law by President Richard Nixon in 1971. You read about many of these in the last two chapters. Write a short summary or timeline from the Russian settlement in Alaska to the signing of the ANCSA.

LEARN MORE

Read more about the Alaska Native Claims Settlement Act by visiting http://www.akhistorycourse.org/modern-alaska/alaska-native-claims-settlement-act

Alaska Native leaders met with then-Secretary of the Interior Walter J. Hickel, far left, to discuss the Alaska land claims dispute in Fall 1970. From left to right: Tim Wallis, President Fairbanks Native Association; Charles Edwardsen, Executive Director Arctic Slope Native Association; Eben Hopson; Emil Notti; attorney Barry Jackson (standing); State Senator William Hensley; and Alfred Ketzler. Farthest back on the right are State Senator Ray Christiansen and Frank Degnan. John Borbridge is seated in the foreground.

UNIT 4: ALASKA LAND IN DISPUTE

LESSON 24: NATIVES MUST PROVE LAND USE

FACTS TO KNOW

Land allotment – A piece of land allocated to an individual or group
Alexander Wilson – Kenaitze Indian tribe member who petitioned for his family's land
Kenaitze Tribe – Tribe of Alaska Natives who lived near the Kenai River

COMPREHENSION QUESTIONS

1) What did Alaska Natives have to prove to the government in order to receive an allotment of land under the Alaska Native Claims Settlement Act? What were some obstacles to doing this?
Alaska's Natives had to show that their ancestors used lands in order to get allotments under the settlement act. This often proved a difficult task, as most of their history was not written down – it passed orally through the generations. When Natives petitioned for land, they had to write detailed accounts of how the land had been used and submit paperwork to the BLM. (Page 240)

2) Summarize Alexander Wilson's account of his ancestors' use of land that he submitted to the government.
Wilson said the Kenaitze lived in a village called Ch-kee-took, upriver from the Kaknu, or Kenai River, where the Federal Aviation Administration and a cannery later stood. He described a place farther upriver where the Natives lived both summer and winter, as well as Portage, which was called Cook-ul-detht. He said white men changed the names to Kenai Lake for the upper body of water and Skilak Lake for the lower. Wilson's account described how his ancestors fished the rivers and hunted for seal and sea lion, which were preserved in blubber or dried. (Pages 240-242)

3) How did/do Alaska Natives view land?
Alaska Natives did (some still do) not view the land as real estate. As the Indian names show, they saw every trail, creek and bend in the river as an individual entity and their connection to the earth ran deep. (Page 241)

4) According to the account given by Alexander Wilson, why did so few Indians know how to read and write their history?
"The reason so few Indians know their background is they were discouraged early in school," he said. "We were broken away from our way of living." He went on to say that

White teachers did not allow the children to speak their Native language, or Russian, in the schoolyard. Teachers punished those speaking anything other than English. "With so few of the older ones left in this village of Kaknu, it is difficult to gather the information needed direct from the older individuals." (Pages 243-244)

5) Did the Wilson family ever receive their family land? Explain why the family strung glass jars around the property?
Wilson died in 1968, but his family carried on with their attempts to claim their ancestral land. Family members applied for one 63-acre piece in the Kenai Lake area and marked the boundary by tying pink fluorescent tape around trees. They then nailed metal screw tops to trees, slipped a paper listing the name of the applicant and the allotment number into a jar, and then screwed the jar onto the nailed lid. Wilson's family only received 13.3 acres of that piece. (Pages 244-245)

DISCUSSION QUESTION

(Discuss this question with your teacher or write your answer in essay form below. Use additional paper if necessary.)

What were some traditions that you learned about in this chapter? Does your family have any traditions? If so, what are they?

_____
_____
_____
_____
_____
_____
_____
_____
_____
_____
_____
_____
_____

LEARN MORE

Read excerpts from *Alaska Native Land Claims,* written by Robert D. Arnold, by visiting http://www.alaskool.org/projects/ancsa/landclaims/LandClaimsTOC.htm

TIME TO REVIEW

Review Chapters 21-24 of your book before moving on the Unit Review. See how many questions you can answer without looking at your book.

Native Land Claims
Word Search Puzzle Key
Find the words listed below

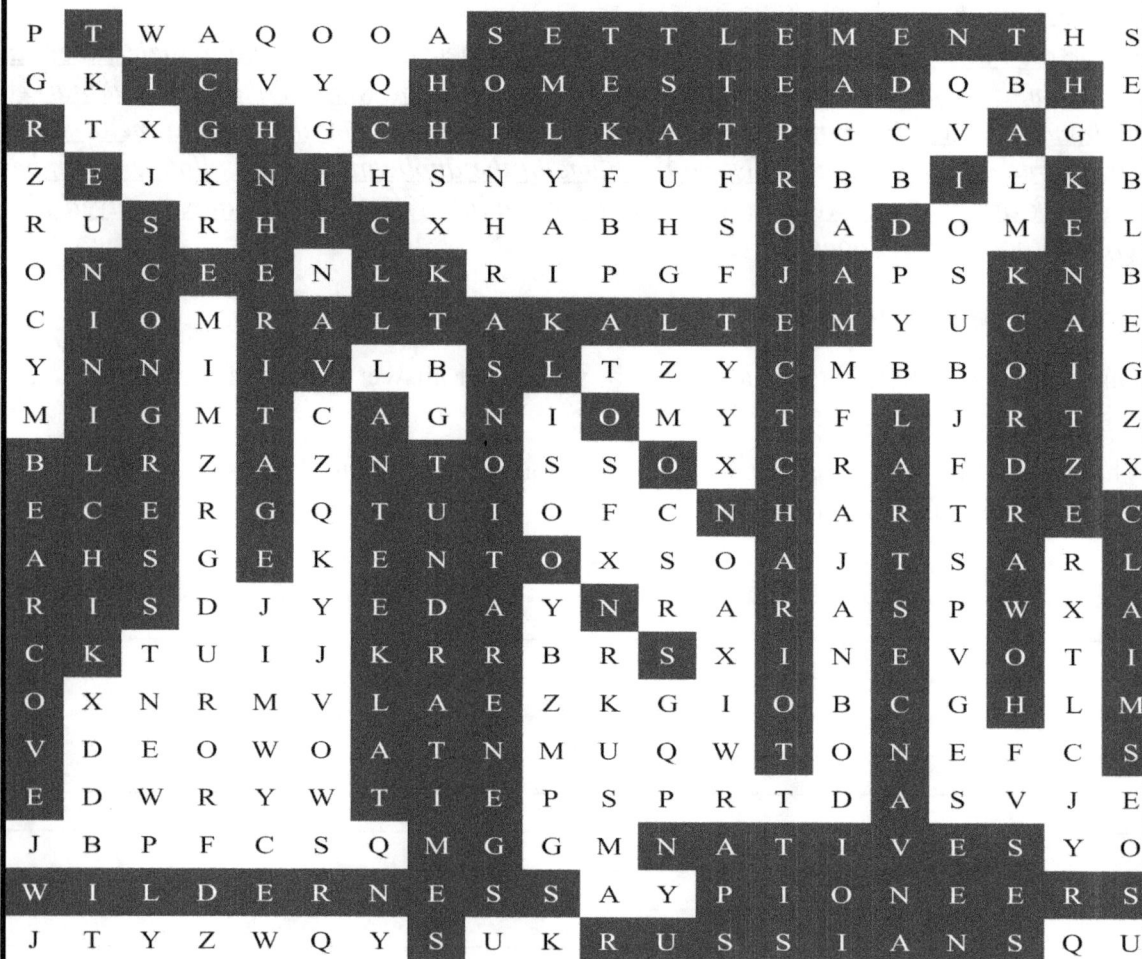

HOMESTEAD	PIONEERS	TALKEETNA
CHICKALOON	BEAR COVE	NINILCHIK
WILDERNESS	TLINGIT	RUSSIANS
CONGRESS	SETTLEMENT	CHILKAT
NATIVES	CLAIMS	HOWARD ROCK
TUNDRA TIMES	PROJECT CHARIOT	HAIDA
RESERVATIONS	ANCESTRAL	HERITAGE
KENAITZE	METLAKATLA	GENERATIONS

UNIT 4: ALASKA LAND IN DISPUTE

REVIEW LESSONS 21-24

Write down what you remember about:

59ers – *Adventurers from Michigan who traveled to Alaska to seek a better life in 1959*

Homestead – *A piece of public land given to settlers for cultivation*

President Abraham Lincoln – *Sixteenth president of the United States who signed the Homestead Act in 1862*

1884 Organic Act – *Provided Alaska its first civilian government and contained language that set the stage for settlement of land claims decades later*

Reservations – *Lands held in trust for Native people by the government*

Land Claim – *Petition to own a segment of land*

Howard Rock – *Founder of the Tundra Times newspaper*

Emil Notti – *Alaska Native leader and activist who fought for Native land rights*

Alaska Federation of Natives – *Statewide organization formed to bring together Natives from dozens of villages and tribes to address land claim issues*

Alaska Native Claims Settlement Act – *Document signed by President Richard Nixon that gave 44 million acres of land and $962.5 million to Alaska Natives*

Land Allotment – *A piece of land allocated to an individual or group*

Alexander Wilson – *Kenaitze Indian tribe member who petitioned for his family's land*

Kenaitze Tribe – *Tribe of Alaska Natives who lived near the Kenai River*

Fill in the blanks

1) A couple of months after Alaska officially became *a state*, an intrepid band adventurers called the "*59ers,*" left *Detroit/Michigan* bound for Alaska. The caravan, consisting of 17 cars, six camper-trailers and a 1936 moving van named "*The Monstrosity*," headed north on March 5, *1959*.

2) In 1862, President *Abraham Lincoln* signed the *Homestead* Act with the idea that free *land* would help develop this unpopulated area. The act took effect on Jan. 1, 1863. Special legislation extended the provisions of the act to the territory of Alaska in *1898*.

3) Life in Alaska proved harder than most expected, though. They encountered many of the same hardships as their *homesteading* brethren of the 19th century, such as *lack of transportation, harsh weather and the dangers posed by wildlife.*

4) Alaska *Natives*, the first to settle the vast unoccupied wilderness of the Great Land thousands of years before Europeans spotted its shores, fought to hold onto *their way of life* for generations. Most had no knowledge that *Russia* had claimed ownership and named it *Russia America* when fur traders landed in the Aleutians in the *1700*s.

5) Even though the *1884 Organic* Act did not have any provisions for Alaska's Natives to gain title to their *land*, it did contain language that would provide for the *land claims settlement* achieved 87 years later.

6) While visiting his family in *Point Hope, Howard Rock* learned that his relatives and friends were worried about a U.S. government plan to *detonate a nuclear blast* and create a harbor in the Arctic for shipping minerals and other goods from northwest Alaska.

7) Environmental studies began to show that fallout from *radiation* after test blasts contaminated lichen, which *caribou* eat, and it was finding its way into humans who consumed the *caribou*. With opposition growing ever stronger, the government backed down and shelved the idea in 1962.

8) The Arctic Slope Native Association asked *Howard Rock* to start the *Tundra Times newspaper*. Along with journalist Tom Snapp, *Rock* covered issues that affected Alaska's Native people and encouraged them to have pride and respect for their *heritage and cultures* – and to *fight* for them.

9) *Howard Rock* helped set the stage for the first *Alaska Federation of Natives* convention in October 1966. More than 400 Alaska Natives representing 17 Native organizations met for three days in *Anchorage* to address their aboriginal *land* rights.

10) U.S. Secretary of the Interior *Stewart Udall* froze Alaska's *land selections* in 1966 until the Native *land claims* issue was settled. *Oil companies* joined Alaska Natives' calls for settling the *land claims* issue following a major discovery of *crude oil* at Prudhoe Bay.

11) When Natives petitioned for *land*, they had to write detailed accounts of *how the land had been used by their ancestors* and submit paperwork to the Bureau of Land Management. One such account, recorded by Kenaitze Indian tribe member *Alexander Wilson* in 1967, described his people's history along the *Kenai* River.

12) Alaska Natives did not view the land as *real estate*. As the Indian names show, they saw every trail, creek and bend in the river as an *individual entity* and their *connection* to the earth ran deep.

13) *Alexander Wilson's* family wrote the information about their Native land *allotment* on a piece of paper, put it into a *Mason jar* and then nailed the *jar* to a tree on the land that had been used by their *ancestors* for generations. *Wilson's* family only received 13.3 acres of that piece.

Alaska's Native people had to prove how their ancestors had used land that they were claiming as the Alaska Native land claims issue made its way through Congress.

UNIT 4: ALASKA LAND IN DISPUTE

UNIT TEST

Choose *two* of the following questions to answer in paragraph form. Use as much detail as possible to completely answer the question.

1) Who were the 59ers? When did they travel to Alaska and why? What challenges did they face when they got there?

2) How did the 1884 Organic Act, the Alaska Statehood Bill and the oil industry all play a part in the signing of the Alaska Native Land Claims Act in 1971?

3) Who was Howard Rock? How did he make a large impact in the Alaska Native communities?

4) Why was Native land claims such a large issue? Why did it take so long to get resolved? How did Native Alaskans view land?

_____
_____
_____
_____
_____
_____
_____
_____
_____
_____
_____
_____
_____
_____
_____
_____
_____
_____
_____
_____
_____
_____
_____

TEACHER NOTES ABOUT THIS UNIT

UNIT 5: PRUDHOE BAY OIL

LESSON 25: BLACK GOLD FOUND ON NORTH SLOPE

FACTS TO KNOW

Prudhoe Bay – Remote area of northern Alaska, called the North Slope, where an immense oil field was discovered in 1967

ARCO – Atlantic Refining and Richfield Oil Company merged to make Atlantic Richfield Oil Company, which made a huge discovery in the North Slope in 1967

John C. "Tennessee" Miller – First to drive vehicles from Fairbanks to the North Slope to prove that a road to the oil fields was possible

COMPREHENSION QUESTIONS

1) How did news of the first tanker leaving the Kenai Peninsula filled with thousands of barrels of oil have a similar effect as news of the *SS Portland* leaving St. Michael with a ton of Klondike gold in 1897?
It had the same effect as the Klondike gold rush. Instead of miners looking for gold, though, it brought prospectors searching for oil. Prospects for the petroleum industry in Alaska by 1966 looked bright. (Page 248)

2) Why did the government limit oil drilling after 30 years of exploration at North Slope reserves?
After 30 years of exploration in the reserve, at a cost of $50 million to $60 million, the federal government finally said enough in 1953 after drilling 75 test wells near Umiat. Congress no longer would appropriate money for a program that was not producing economically viable results. (Page 251)

3) In what other ways did the government limit oil drilling?
In December 1960, the government made the area for finding commercial deposits of oil even smaller after it established the Arctic National Wildlife Refuge, which covered almost 19 million acres. Between the refuge and the naval reserve, the oil industry now was limited to exploring acreage lying between the Colville and Canning rivers. (Page 252)

4) What were some obstacles to exploring for oil in Alaska?
Drilling on Naval Petroleum Reserve No. 4 had shown those sediments contained both oil and gas. Experts just did not know if the area had "favorable reservoir conditions," which are so essential for major accumulations of oil or gas. Transportation to the remote region was problematic, as well. There were no roads to the potentially oil-rich land, and passage via ship to Point Barrow was limited to a few weeks a year due to sea ice. (Page 253)

5) What major discovery did ARCO and Humble Oil make in December 1967?
ARCO partnered with Humble Oil, and the companies began sharing maps and expertise to decide the most promising spots to sink test wells. Then 11 years after hitting its first producing well on Swanson River, ARCO hit the mother lode of crude along the Beaufort Sea coast on Alaska's North Slope. (Page 255)

6) Why did oil company executives from all over the world meet in Anchorage in 1969?
Oil companies, investors, state officials and more than 150 accredited newsmen representing newspapers, magazines, radio and television from all parts of the world filled the Sydney Laurence Auditorium on Sept. 10, 1969, to bid on land leases near the Prudhoe Bay oil discoveries. (Pages 257-259)

DISCUSSION QUESTION

(Discuss this question with your teacher or write your answer in essay form below. Use additional paper if necessary.)

Why did oil companies need to keep their oil discoveries secret?

_____
_____
_____
_____
_____
_____
_____
_____
_____
_____
_____
_____
_____
_____
_____

ENRICHMENT ACTIVITY

Visit http://www.akhistorycourse.org/comic/AK_Economy_pp1-55.pdf to read an online comic book about the discovery of oil in Alaska and other adventures in Alaska's economy. Be prepared to make your own comic book in the next lesson.

LEARN MORE

Learn more about oil discovery and development in Alaska by visiting http://www.akhistorycourse.org/modern-alaska/oil-discovery-and-development-in-alaska

UNIT 5: PRUDHOE BAY OIL

LESSON 26: DEADHORSE RISES IN THE ARCTIC

FACTS TO KNOW

H.C. "Harry" Jamison – Richfield Oil's exploration supervisor for Alaska
Deadhorse – Land base on the North Slope built to house personnel and provide support for drilling operations
Prudhoe Unit – Merger of 16 oil companies that managed operations on the North Slope

COMPREHENSION QUESTIONS

1) According to oil executive Harry Jamison, what were the oil companies scrambling to do after the oil boom began?
He said they had to meet the immediate demand for action on the Slope, extension wells, airstrip construction and controls, camp expansion, construction equipment, additional aircraft, fuel supplies, seismic crews, drilling rigs, security measures and a hundred other things. "What about housing several hundred, then several thousand workers? What about flying them in and out? What about finding them in the first place?" he said. (Page 262)

2) How did oil companies meet some of these needs?
They built a land base on the North Slope to house personnel and provide support for drilling operations, 206 miles southeast of Barrow. It became known as Deadhorse. It was a marvel of modern engineering and eventually encompassed 29 square miles of land and 3 square miles of water. (Pages 262-263)

3) What other problem did the oil prospectors face during this time? How did they solve this problem?
The State of Alaska required that the Prudhoe Bay oil field be developed as one unit, not individually by the various companies that held the leases. The 16 oil companies decided to have two companies manage the operations on the North Slope. The unusual agreement between all these companies, called The Prudhoe Unit, formed two areas within the huge oil field – one for gas and one for oil. ARCO operated the eastern side and BP operated the west side. (Pages 263-264)

4) Why wasn't the pipeline built immediately after the signing of the Alaska Native Land Claims Act? How did the building of the pipeline help Alaska's economy?
Even after the Alaska Native Claims Settlement Act was passed in 1971, it took a few more years for the dust to settle between Congress, federal agencies, the state and

environmentalists before the oil industry actually began construction on that project. Unemployment numbers were up 20 percent from the year before as workers were lured north by a 'boom' initiated by the developing North Slope oil fields. (Pages 266-267)

DISCUSSION QUESTION

(Discuss this question with your teacher or write your answer in essay form below. Use additional paper if necessary.)

How did the discovery of oil change the history of Alaska – both positively and negatively?

_____
_____
_____
_____
_____
_____
_____
_____
_____
_____
_____
_____
_____
_____
_____
_____
_____
_____
_____

ENRICHMENT ACTIVITY

Create your own comic book or short story surrounding an adventure in Alaska's economy. Include some of the history that you are learning about in this unit. You will have the rest of this unit to complete your story.

LEARN MORE

Read more about the importance of oil to Alaska's economy by visiting http://www.akhistorycourse.org/modern-alaska/alaska-yesterday-today-and-tomorrow/alaska-economy-and-resource-development

UNIT 5: PRUDHOE BAY OIL

LESSON 27: PLANS FOR A PIPELINE PROGRESS

FACTS TO KNOW

Trans-Alaska Pipeline System – Joint venture between six major oil companies
Environmentalists – Activists who focus on protecting the earth and natural resources

COMPREHENSION QUESTIONS

1) What were some of the ways that oil companies considered transporting oil from the North Slope to market?
Some thought it could be transported by giant tankers or oil-carrying submarines. Some thought a 2,900-mile pipeline across Canada to the Midwest might be the answer. Yet others believed an 800-mile line south to an ice-free port in Southern Alaska, where ocean-going oil tankers could be filled, would be the best bet. One company suggested nuclear-powered submarine tankers. Others pitched the idea of building a railroad from Prudhoe Bay to Alberta, Canada, where pipeline facilities already existed. (Page 268)

2) Which two ideas proved to be the most popular? Which one was chosen and why?
When the air cleared, two pipeline ideas proved most popular. One from Prudhoe Bay south to Valdez, or one that ran from the North Slope into Canada, via the Mackenzie River Valley to Alberta, to connect to the existing pipeline system that went over to Chicago and the Great Lakes industrial belt. Alaska Gov. Keith Miller and most Alaskans recognized the benefits for Alaska with building an all-Alaska pipeline south and agreed with the proposal to build a terminal in Valdez. (Pages 268-269)

3) Why did Native villages file suit to halt construction of the pipeline?
Native villages filed suit in federal court to halt construction of a haul road to the North Slope, as it and a pipeline would go across land they claimed was ancestral. The people of Stevens Village said, "we can't let this happen. That until our claims are settled, until we have certainty about what we own and what we don't own and how this will affect us and our children, we can't allow this to happen." (Page 271)

4) Why did environmental conservation groups file suit to halt the construction of the pipeline?
Three conservation groups – Wilderness Society, Friends of the Earth and the Environmental Defense Fund Inc. – also filed a federal suit asking the U.S. District Court to bar construction of the pipeline. Environmentalists were worried that the oil industry would dig trenches and bury pipe just like they had all around the world. They believed that

approach would harm Alaska's delicate arctic region where permafrost would be melted by hot-oil pipes and cause massive environmental damage. (Pages 270-273)

5) Why was there pressure for a domestic source of oil in 1973?
In retaliation for American support of Israel in the Yom Kippur War, Arab states declared an embargo on oil shipments to America. That tipped the balance in favor of a new domestic source of oil. Democratic Sen. Henry Jackson of Washington believed that America was importing too much oil from overseas, which subjected the United States to blackmail. (Page 274)

6) When was construction of the pipeline finally authorized? When did construction for the pipeline begin?
President Nixon signed the Trans-Alaska Pipeline Authorization Act on Nov. 16, 1973. The act was intended "to ensure that, because of ... the national interest in early delivery of North Slope oil to domestic markets, the trans-Alaska oil pipeline be constructed promptly without further administrative or judicial delay or impediment." The act directed Secretary of the Interior Morton to authorize the federal right of way for the pipeline, which he signed on Jan. 23, 1974. The state followed suit four months later, and issued its right of way lease on May 3. (Page 274)

DISCUSSION QUESTION

(Discuss this question with your teacher or write your answer in essay form below. Use additional paper if necessary.)

How did the discovery of oil change Alaska's society?

___
___
___
___
___

ENRICHMENT ACTIVITY

Continue creating your own comic book or short story surrounding an adventure in Alaska's economy. Remember to include some of the history that you are learning about in this unit. You will have the rest of this unit to complete your story.

LEARN MORE

Look for this book at your local library: *Amazing Pipeline Stories: How Building the trans-Alaska Pipeline Transformed Life on America's Last Frontier*. Dermot Cole. Epicenter Press, 1997.

UNIT 5: PRUDHOE BAY OIL

LESSON 28: PIPELINE SNAKES ACROSS ALASKA

FACTS TO KNOW

Alyeska Service Company – Managed the construction of the pipeline
Frank Moolin – Senior project manager on the pipeline known for his work ethic
ARCO Juneau – First oil tanker to take Prudhoe Bay oil to the Lower 48 on Aug. 1, 1977

COMPREHENSION QUESTIONS

1) What were some design features that were included in the pipeline plans to meet the special challenges of transporting oil through Alaska's unique environment?
Experts studied the best way to cross three mountain ranges – the Brooks, Alaska and Chugach – and hundreds of streams and rivers. The final design made sure the line could withstand a magnitude 8.5 Richter Scale earthquake, too, as the pipe would cross three faults – Denali, McGinnis Glacier and Donnelly Dome. Along with many other considerations, the planners noted the pipe would be buried wherever possible, bypass geologic hazards and population centers, be raised above permafrost where needed and avoid sites of antiquities and important fish-spawning or wildlife areas. (Pages 282-283)

2) What was life like for those working on the pipeline?
Every worker was guaranteed 40 hours per week of pay, even if they couldn't work due to bad weather. Alyeska not only paid high wages, it provided the best food and housing and other amenities to keep its labor force happy. Workers on average spent a week on and a week off, or two weeks on and two weeks off, laboring 12 hours a day, seven days a week in a nearly flat, treeless land to build the pipeline. (Pages 298-310)

3) Describe the steps needed to lay the pipe for the trans-Alaska oil pipeline.
The right of way first needed to be cleared with chainsaws, bulldozers and scrapers that followed a roughly laid out previously surveyed route. Then a group of surveyors and engineers followed to see if the pipeline could go in that spot or if soil conditions necessitated it be moved to another. Once a section was deemed fit, augers and drillers made holes for foundations for supports to hold the pipe if it was to be placed above ground. Other crews filled the holes with water and dirt, which froze solid, to hold the semi-circular supports in place. Next the pipeline sections were carried in 40- or 80-foot segments by crane or sideboom to the location, lowered into place and welded together. (Pages 295-296)

4) How did the building of the pipeline increase crime in Fairbanks?
When workers went off duty they headed to the city and spent their hard-earned wages with abandon, and crime rates increased dramatically. According to Fairbanks police officer J.B. Carnahan, "people coming to town with three, four, five thousand dollars of cash in their pockets. Suddenly, women that we'd never seen around town before were appearing from places like Florida and New York and suddenly we had reports of gambling going on." Major organized crime also found its way to Alaska. Newspapers covered many stories about gambling and prostitution. (Pages 299-300)

5) Was work on the pipeline dangerous? Explain your answer.
Yes. During its construction, 32 Alyeska Pipeline Service Co. employees or contract workers died. Most were killed in 10 aircraft crashes. In addition, three men died when a Hovercraft crashed; two men walked into helicopter blades; one was crushed between a forklift truck and its load; two drowned in the cement they were pouring for a building; and another was killed during a seismic survey. Many other workers suffered serious injuries from accidents on drilling rigs, through snow blindness and severe frostbite. (Page 309)

6) When was the pipeline completed? Describe the impact that it had on Alaska.
The last pipeline weld was made at Pump Station No. 3, near Atigun Pass, to finish the project on May 31, 1977. "Alaskan oil has been the biggest resource bonanza in U.S. history, transforming Alaska from one of the poorest to one of the wealthiest states in the nation," Byron Mallot said. Nearly one-tenth of the crude oil used in America flowed through that pipeline. It moved its billionth barrel of oil in early 1980, and for decades royalties provided 80-85 percent of the state's operating budget. (Pages 309-311)

DISCUSSION QUESTION

(Discuss this question with your teacher or write your answer in essay form below. Use additional paper if necessary.)

How do you think Alaska would be different if the discovery of oil never happened?

_____
_____
_____
_____
_____
_____

ENRICHMENT ACTIVITY

Finish your own comic book or short story surrounding an adventure in Alaska's economy. Once completed, share it with your teacher and/or your class.

LEARN MORE

Take a video tour of the Alaska pipeline by visiting https://www.youtube.com/watch?v=_OrAmGOFOEk

TIME TO REVIEW

Review Chapters 25-28 of your book before moving on the Unit Review. See how many questions you can answer without looking at your book.

This photograph shows construction of the pipeline up and over the Chugach Mountains on its way to Valdez. The Alyeska Pipeline Service Company said they installed 80 mechanical check valves at up-hill sections along the pipeline that close automatically in the event of a pressure loss in the line upstream of the valve. These valves prevent the flow of oil in the wrong direction back down the 48-inch-diameter pipe.

UNIT 5: PRUDHOE BAY OIL

REVIEW LESSONS 25-28

Write down what you remember about:

Prudhoe Bay – *Remote area of northern Alaska, called the North Slope, where an immense oil field was discovered in 1967*

ARCO – *Atlantic Refining and Richfield Oil Company merged to make Atlantic Richfield Oil Company, which made a huge discovery in the North Slope in 1967*

John C. "Tennessee" Miller – *First to drive vehicles from Fairbanks to the North Slope to prove that a road to the oil fields was possible*

H.C. "Harry" Jamison – *Richfield Oil's exploration supervisor for Alaska*

Deadhorse – *Land base on the North Slope built to house personnel and provide support for drilling operations*

Prudhoe Unit – *Merger of 16 oil companies that managed operations on the North Slope*

Trans-Alaska Pipeline System – *Joint venture between six major oil companies*

Environmentalists – *Activists who focus on protecting the earth and natural resources*

Alyeska Service Company – *Managed the construction of the pipeline*

Frank Moolin – *Senior project manager on the pipeline known for his work ethic*

ARCO Juneau – *First oil tanker to take Prudhoe Bay oil to the Lower 48 on Aug. 1, 1977*

Fill in the blanks

1) News of the first tanker, *F.S. Bryant*, leaving the *Kenai* Peninsula filled with thousands of barrels of oil bound for the *Lower 48* may be compared to the news of the SS *Portland* leaving St. Michael with its ton of *Klondike gold* in 1897. It had the same effect. Instead of miners looking for *gold*, though, it brought *prospectors* searching for oil.

2) Geologists believed that Alaska's *Arctic Slope* held the greatest petroleum potential because of its *vast basin* with tremendous thickness of *marine sediments*. Drilling done on Naval Petroleum Reserve No. 4 had shown those sediments contained both *oil* and *gas*. Exploration moved slowly due to problems with drilling and production in such a *remote, frigid* region. There were no *roads* to the potentially oil-rich land, and passage via *ship* to Point Barrow was limited to a few weeks a year due to sea ice.

3) In 1966, the federal government put a stop to Alaska choosing any more *land* from the 103 million acres granted it under the *Alaska Statehood* Act. U.S. Interior Secretary *Stewart Udall* imposed a "*land freeze*" on the transfer of *lands* claimed by *Alaska Natives* until Congress sorted out their claims.

4) Once the huge oil field was discovered in *Prudhoe Bay* in 1968, the race was on to build the infrastructure needed to develop the resource. The land base that grew on the *North Slope* to house personnel and provide support for drilling operations, 206 miles southeast of Barrow, became known as *Deadhorse*.

5) The 16 *oil companies* decided to have two companies manage the operations on the *North Slope*. The unusual agreement between all these companies, called *The Prudhoe Unit*, formed two areas within the huge oil field – one for *oil* and one for *gas*.

6) Alaska Gov. Keith Miller and most Alaskans recognized the benefits for Alaska with building an all-Alaska *pipeline* in the *south* and agreed with the proposal to build a terminal in *Valdez*.

7) Although oil companies were not given the green light to build the *pipeline* until 1974, they laid much of the groundwork in advance. In October 1968, three *major oil companies* formed a joint venture to *organize, design and plan the pipeline* to transport oil from *Prudhoe Bay* to market as soon as all the legal hurdles had been addressed. The new enterprise was called *Trans-Alaska Pipeline System*.

8) *Environmentalists* wanted to limit development in Alaska's northern *wilderness*, but many Alaskans thought they had enough *wilderness* areas in the vast state and developing the *North Slope* could be done in an environmentally responsible way.

9) The battle over building the *pipeline* continued until October 1973 when, in retaliation for American support of *Israel* in the *Yom Kippur* War, Arab states declared an embargo on *oil shipments* to America. That tipped the balance in favor of a new *domestic source* of oil rather than importing so much oil from overseas.

10) The eight-member Trans-Alaska Pipeline System created the *Alyeska Pipeline Service Company* to oversee construction activities for the massive project. *Alyeska* then developed the pipeline *design and specifications* in coordination with many federal and state agencies.

11) *Alyeska* altered its plans as it performed tests on everything from the *earthquake* zones to *perma*frost. After its analysis was complete, the industry decided the best route would take the pipeline through Dietrich Pass, later named *Atigun* Pass, on to *Rampart* Canyon and Thompson Pass to *Valdez*.

12) Every pipeline worker was guaranteed *40 hours* per week of pay, even if they couldn't work due to *bad weather*. *Alyeska* not only paid *high* wages, it provided the best *food and housing* and other amenities to keep its labor force happy. Those *high* wages created a boomtown atmosphere in both Fairbanks and Anchorage. This also increased *crime* in these cities.

13) When completed in *1977*, the pipeline crossed 34 *major rivers*, around 800 smaller *streams* and three *mountain* ranges. It also had 11 *pumping* stations to help move the oil along. The *Valdez Marine Terminal* was built at the southern end of the pipeline.

14) According to Native leader *Byron Mallot*, the pipeline, which has delivered billions of barrels of oil, has had some spills from *accidents, vandalism, permafrost thaws and some corrosion due to aging*. But overall, it has worked as well as most everyone could have hoped. Alaska oil has been the *biggest resource bonanza* in U.S. history, transforming Alaska from one of the *poorest* to one of the *wealthiest* states in the nation.

Alaska Oil Pipeline
Word Scramble Key
Please unscramble the words below

#	Scrambled	Answer	Clue
1.	dsaordeeh	deadhorse	Large land base on Alaska's North Slope where workers live
2.	udrphoe yba	prudhoe bay	An immense oil field was discovered here in 1967
3.	anyrtb	bryant	Name of oil tanker that carried the first shipment of oil out of the Kenai Peninsula
4.	mot maarllhs	tom marshall	Alaska's only geologist in 1964
5.	rcedu oil	crude oil	Alaskans call this "black gold"
6.	dilirlng rgi	drilling rig	Name for equipment that digs down into the earth to find oil
7.	feruotab esa	beaufort sea	Large body of water at North Slope
8.	eazvdl	valdez	Southern port where trans-Alaska oil pipeline ends
9.	ltoadn	dalton	Name of haul road to North Slope
10.	ayalesk	alyeska	Service company that oversaw the Alaska pipeline construction activities
11.	pigs	pigs	equipment that goes through the pipeline to clean and gather information
12.	auujne	juneau	First Prudhoe Bay oil left on this tanker in 1977

UNIT 5: PRUDHOE BAY OIL

UNIT TEST

Choose *two* of the following questions to answer in paragraph form. Use as much detail as possible to completely answer the question.

1) Describe the impact that the petroleum boom in Alaska had on its population, society, government and economy.

2) Name two ways the construction of the pipeline was delayed. How were these issues resolved?

3) What were some of the obstacles to drilling and transporting oil through Alaska for market?

4) What was life like for the construction workers who built the pipeline? What kind of hours did they work? Did they make good money? Was it dangerous work?

TEACHER NOTES ABOUT THIS UNIT

UNIT 6: SOME HIGHLIGHTS

LESSON 29: ICEWORM REVIVES CORDOVA

FACTS TO KNOW

Cordova – Small town in Prince William Sound that used the idea of an iceworm to combat mid-winter doldrums and draw tourists to town
Iceworm – Tiny black worms that avoid the sun and spend their lives in glacial ice
Ohmer Waer – Hotel manager in Cordova who had the idea of creating an "iceworm"

COMPREHENSION QUESTIONS

1) Why did Dawson newspaper man E.J. White write an article about iceworms one winter during the Klondike gold rush?
His invention was the result of a dearth of news in Dawson and a demand from his editor to go out and rustle up some. "Get me something that will make headlines and sell papers," the editor of the Klondike Nugget told him. As White pondered what sort of news might attract readers, a huge storm hit the Canadian gold-rush town. That's when a great idea hit the newsman. He announced that new creatures had emerged after the storm: ice worms. (Page 313)

2) Did E.J. White make up the idea of iceworms, or do iceworms really exist? Explain your answer.
Although many people believe ice worms are fantasy, they do, indeed, exist and were first discovered in 1887 on Alaska's Muir Glacier. The tiny black worms avoid the sun and spend their lives in glacial ice. They creep onto the surface of glaciers at night and retreat underneath the ice before dawn. (Page 314)

3) What organization did Ohmer Waer, Bob Logan, Frank Smith and Harold Bonser form in 1960?
They formed the Cordova Visitors Association. (Page 315)

4) Describe the design of the iceworm that Cordova residents created.
In 1960 just about everyone in town pitched in and did their bit, Waer said. Robert Banta, owner of Banta's Builders Supply, made rings of oak for the body. Banta called Ohmer down to his shop one day to look at some aluminized nine-foot-wide cotton cloth. He said he could supply 150 feet of it, so soon the town women were busy working on the cover for the body of the Iceworm. It takes eight legs to carry the huge head – two more every so often and four under the tail. (Pages 315-316)

5) How do Cordovans use the iceworm to celebrate their city?

Visitors have come to the winter festival, held the end of January or beginning of February, from all around the world. The "Iceworm coin," a wooden buck accepted in payment for purchases, is now a collector's item found in many European cities – a few have even reached Cordoba, Spain, the city for which Cordova is named. Cordovans celebrate their Iceworm Festival to this day. (Page 317)

DISCUSSION QUESTION

(Discuss this question with your teacher or write your answer in essay form below. Use additional paper if necessary.)

What do you think the creation of the Iceworm Festival did for the residents of Cordova?

_____
_____
_____
_____
_____
_____
_____
_____
_____
_____
_____
_____
_____
_____
_____
_____
_____

ENRICHMENT ACTIVITY

Classroom Teachers: This project can be done individually or in small groups.

You have just been put in charge of your city's visitors' association. Come up with a creative festival to draw tourists to your city and teach them more about it. Write out your plans or create a poster to advertise the festival.

LEARN MORE

Read more about art, culture, and recreation in various Alaskan cities by visiting http://www.akhistorycourse.org/americas-territory/alaskas-heritage/chapter-4-19-art-literature-science-cultural-institutions-and-recreation

UNIT 6: SOME HIGHLIGHTS

LESSON 30: THE PAINTING PACHYDERM
LESSON 31: BETTY THE FIRETRUCK

Note: Read both chapters 30 and 31 before completing this lesson.

FACTS TO KNOW

Pachyderm – Thick-skinned, hoofed mammal such as an elephant
Annabelle – Elephant that arrived in Anchorage in 1966
Alaska Zoo – Anchorage zoo started by Sammye Seawell, caretaker of Annabelle
Homer – City overlooking Kachemak Bay on the Kenai Peninsula
General Mills – National company that offered a program to exchange coupons for household items

COMPREHENSION QUESTIONS

1) Explain how Annabelle become the first pachyderm in Alaska since the ice age.
It all started when Jack Snyder saw a tongue-in-cheek ad for a Chiffon toilet paper contest for grocers in 1966. The Crown Zellerbach company announced: "$3,000 or a baby elephant" to the winner. The Anchorage grocer won the contest. Snyder then startled the tissue paper executives when he said, "I'll take the elephant." (Page 318)

2) How did Sammye Seawell come up with the idea to start the Alaska Zoo?
Annabelle became quite popular with Anchorage residents, which sparked an idea that would secure Annabelle's future. Seawell persuaded Anchorage residents to form a non-profit corporation to build a place "where the public could visit animals and learn about them." (Page 319)

3) What special talent allowed Annabelle to raise several hundred thousand dollars for the zoo? How did her trainers discover and develop this talent?
Something magical happened at America's farthest-north zoo when trainers put a paintbrush into Annabelle's trunk in 1991. She started splattering brush strokes across canvas and created paintings in front of cheering visitors. Her prints raised several hundred thousand dollars for the zoo. Her art also graced note cards and coffee mugs. (Page 321)

4) What item did the residents of Homer receive for participating in General Mills coupon program? How many coupons did they need to collect for this item?
The Homer fire department needed a firetruck. They needed five million coupons, which equaled about $25,000 in 1969 – more than $162,000 in 2015 dollars. (Page 322)

5) How did the residents of Homer know that this was possible?
Homer residents knew it was possible, because another Alaska community had saved General Mills coupons in 1964 for a vehicle. The Copper Valley School in Glennallen organized a campaign and collected 1.5 million coupons to trade in for a new school bus. (Pages 322-323)

6) According to *Fire Chief Kranich*, the "Betty" firetruck story represented a time of *independence* in the community. "In times past, the *government* didn't do for the people, the people did for themselves," he said.

DISCUSSION QUESTION

(Discuss this question with your teacher or write your answer in essay form below. Use additional paper if necessary.)

How did children in Anchorage play a part in the opening of the Alaska Zoo?

_____
_____
_____
_____
_____
_____
_____
_____
_____
_____
_____
_____
_____
_____
_____
_____
_____
_____
_____

ENRICHMENT ACTIVITY

Check in on the polar bears at the Alaska Zoo by going to the live bear cam at http://alaskazoo.org/live-polar-bear-camera. Take a field trip to the Alaska Zoo in Anchorage and check out all the animals that call the zoo home.

LEARN MORE

Learn more about the Alaska Zoo by visiting http://www.alaskazoo.org/

UNIT 6: SOME HIGHLIGHTS

LESSON 32: A GREAT RACE IS BORN

FACTS TO KNOW

Dorothy Page – Secretary of Aurora Dog Mushers Club who had the idea for an annual Iditarod Trail race

Joe Redington Sr. – Veteran dog musher who became known as the "father of the Iditarod"

Iditarod Trail – Historic trail that runs from Seward to Nome; the annual race runs from Willow to Nome

Dick Wilmarth – Gold miner who won the 1973 Iditarod Trail Race

COMPREHENSION QUESTIONS

1) How did Dorothy Page come up with the idea for the Iditarod Trail Race? Why?
She saw that snowmachines were taking the place of dog teams and mushing. She thought a sled dog race on the historic Iditarod Trail might revitalize a longtime Alaska tradition. She talked to Joe Redington Sr. about her idea during a break at the Willow Winter Carnival sled dog races in 1966. (Page 327)

2) When was the inaugural (first) race? What happened to delay the race for 4 more years?
Fifty-eight mushers signed up to compete for $25,000 in prize money for the 1967 inaugural race. Since only nine miles of the trail had been cleared, the race ran from Knik to Big Lake on Saturday, and from Big Lake to Knik on Sunday, for a total of 56 miles. Due to a lack of snow in 1968, a lack of money in 1969 and a lack of interest from 1970 to 1972, the race was put on hold. (Page 328)

3) How did Dick Wilmarth describe the race?
He later told reporters he heard some of his competitors talking about quitting about halfway to Nome. They told him they wanted to quit the race, but they wanted the decision to be unanimous. Wilmarth was not a quitter and he told them he was headed to Nome. The determined musher, who snared beaver for food along the trail, said people along the Yukon did not want to share food or fish with him. Wilmarth crossed the finish line first and collected $12,000 in prize money. (Pages 329-330)

4) How has the race changed over the years?
Alternating every year between the southern route and the northern route, the current trails cross the Alaska Range, Kuskokwim Mountains, Nulato Hills and more than 200 miles along the mighty Yukon River. By the early 1980s, the prize money had doubled and the trail time had dropped almost in half. (Page 331)

DISCUSSION QUESTION

(Discuss this question with your teacher or write your answer in essay form below. Use additional paper if necessary.)

What advantages did Dick Wilmarth have over the other mushers in the race?

_____
_____
_____
_____
_____
_____
_____
_____
_____
_____
_____
_____
_____
_____
_____
_____
_____
_____
_____
_____

LEARN MORE

Read more about Iditarod Trail Race musher George Attla by finding this book at your library: *Everything I Know About Training and Racing Sled Dogs.* George Attla. Rome, New York: Arner Publications, 1974.

MAP ACTIVITY

Locate the following important Ititarod Trails towns/stops/bodies of water along the Northern and Southern routes of the Last Great Race:

1) Iditarod 2) Koyuk 3) Grayling 4) Nikolai 5) Anchorage 6) Ruby
7) Bering Sea 8) Kaltag 9) Wasilla 10) Shaktoolik 11) Willow 12) Ophir
13) Rainy Pass 14) Nome 15) Norton Sound

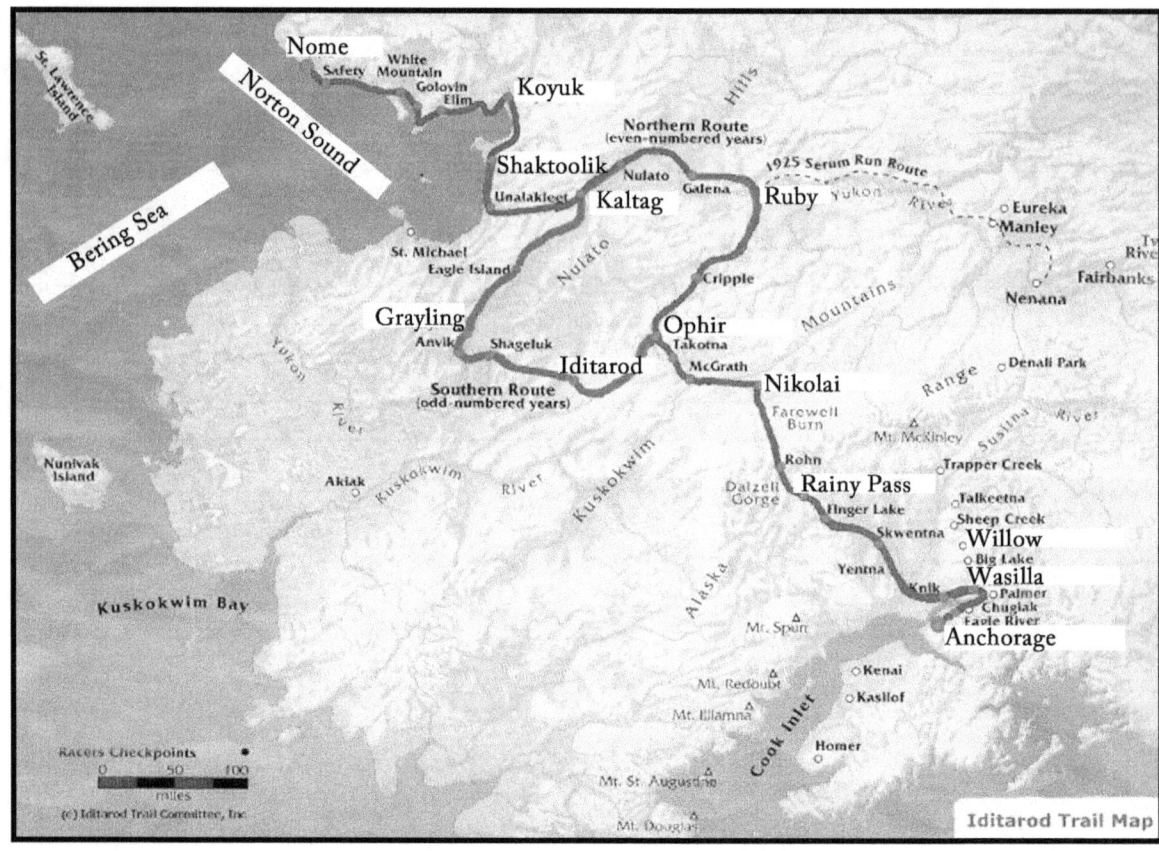

Some Highlights
Word Scramble Puzzle Key
Unscramble the words below

#	Scrambled	Answer	Clue
1.	riecwmo	iceworm	It lives in glacial ice and hides from sunlight
2.	oorcdav	cordova	Town in Prince William Sound that holds a winter festival
3.	sleicrag	glaciers	Massive frozen rivers of ice
4.	nebaelanl	annabelle	Name of elephant that arrived in Alaska in 1960s
5.	aaaslk ooz	alaska zoo	An animal facility in Anchorage changed its name to this in June 1980
6.	pahymercd	pachyderm	An elephant is this type of mammal
7.	smemay slaewle	sammye seawell	She was instrumental in getting a home for animals started Anchorage in the 1960s
8.	ohmer	homer	Town in Kachemak Bay that needed an emergency vehicle in the 1960s
9.	tybet	betty	What people named the emergency vehicle that they obtained in a unique way
10.	coonspu	coupons	Townspeople saved millions of these in order to get an emergency vehicle
11.	rkfertcui	firetruck	The type of emergency vehicle needed in a Kachemak Bay town in the 1960s
12.	iodidtar	iditarod	This is also called "The Last Great Race"

UNIT 7: SOME LOW POINTS

LESSON 33: CORDOVA BURNS

FACTS TO KNOW

Prince William Sound – Cordova, devastated by fire in May 1963, is located on this sound in the Gulf of Alaska on the east side of the Kenai Peninsula

Kennecott Copper Mines – At one time it was the largest copper mine in the world until it closed in 1938

COMPREHENSION QUESTIONS

1) What "almost fatal blow" did Cordova experience in 1938? What resource helped it bounce back?
In 1938, the Kennecott copper mines closed down. The railroad was abandoned, the rails sold for scrap and ghost towns were left scattered along the 200-mile right of way. Cordova had another resource to fall back on – fishing and canning fish, clams and crab provided employment for the people who stayed with the town. (Page 332)

2) Where did the fire start? How did the firemen attempt to stop the spread of the fire?
It started in the Club Café in the Van Brocklin Building and quickly spread through the Club Bar and Cordova Commercial Company on the corner of First and Council streets, according to Cordova historian Dixie Lambert. Firemen had used the practice of lighting dynamite in burning buildings in the past to stop the spread of fire, but the strategy did not work this time. The six charges of dynamite only added to the confusion. (Pages 333-334)

3) How much damage did the fire cause?
The fire did not stop until 14 downtown buildings had been destroyed and many more damaged, including City Hall, the fire department, Cordova Cleaners and First Bank of Cordova. (Page 335)

4) How did many Cordovans react as the fire was spreading? How was their reaction different by 12:30p.m.?
At the height of the excitement, everyone was too busy to feel the full impact of the catastrophe. Victims even joked with one another as they staggered out of fire-threatened apartments and stores under huge loads of clothing, bedding, furniture, household goods, gill nets, outboard motors and merchandise. They were relieved that no one had been seriously injured and could even see humor. By 12:30 p.m., with the fire under control, reaction set in. The tired, lined faces of Cordova's weary citizens showed that they now

realized their loss. They also realized that if they were to survive this blow, they faced the fight of their lives. (Pages 335-336)

5) What were some of the groups that assisted Cordova after the fire?
The Small Business Bureau helped arrange loans to the business people to rebuild. The American Red Cross and The Salvation Army offered assistance to the displaced residents. The Alaska Railroad sped supplies from Anchorage to Seward and the Alaska Steamship Company transported them to Cordova. Those from other towns donated clothing and household goods that were flown into Cordova from Kodiak, Juneau and Anchorage. The Alaska Communications System donated telephone equipment. (Page 336)

DISCUSSION QUESTION

(Discuss this question with your teacher or write your answer in essay form below. Use additional paper if necessary.)

What did Gov. William Egan say about Cordova when he came to survey the damage a few days after the fire?

_____
_____
_____
_____
_____
_____
_____
_____
_____
_____
_____
_____
_____
_____

ENRICHMENT ACTIVITY

Watch this short video to learn more about the salmon industry in Cordova:
https://www.youtube.com/watch?v=u_aIGVqKItw

LEARN MORE

Look for this book at your local library:
From Fish and Copper: Cordova's Heritage and Buildings. Nielsen, Nikki. Anchorage: Cordova Historical Society, 1984.

UNIT 7: SOME LOW POINTS

LESSON 34: FLOODWATERS FILL FAIRBANKS

FACTS TO KNOW

Chena River – Fairbanks river that flooded in August 1967

Fairbanks – Large city in the interior of Alaska that experienced massive flooding in the summer of 1967

Flood Control Act of 1968 – Largest federal civil works program in the state, created to prevent future flooding in the Fairbanks area

COMPREHENSION QUESTIONS

1) What were many Fairbanks residents doing as rain began to fall in July 1967?
Most were in the midst of the Alaska Purchase Centennial, celebrating the U.S. purchase of Alaska from Russia in 1867. (Page 336)

2) Describe what Sandy Vernon and her husband did when the floodwaters got to their house.
The couple could not get their car out of the driveway before rushing water filled the street. "We began walking in the dark in waist-deep water. We were hit by debris spinning in the still rising waters." The couple felt their way by foot along the ties of an Alaska Railroad track bed, not knowing that the water was washing away the gravel underneath the ties. Vernon and her husband hopped aboard a fire truck and were taken with about a dozen others to the FE Gold Camp. (Pages 340-341)

3) What conditions made the rescue mission difficult?
The city became a five-mile-wide lake of deep, sludgy water filled with lost property covered with sewage and garbage. The flood knocked out power, communications, water and sewer utilities. It washed away roads, bridges and rails, too, which isolated Fairbanks and made rescue efforts difficult. (Page 341)

4) Where did many Fairbanks residents take shelter after the flood?
People with apartments made room and shared dry living spaces with those in need. They pooled food and cooked large meals for the crowd gathered in Fairbanks' only "skyscraper." They ferried most of those found to the University of Alaska, which sat on College Hill, safe from the flood. (Page 344)

5) How much damage did the flood do? Were there any casualties?
The flood of 1967, killed seven and caused more than $200 million ($1.4 billion in 2015 dollars) in damage. (Page 348)

DISCUSSION QUESTION

(Discuss this question with your teacher or write your answer in essay form below. Use additional paper if necessary.)

Do you remember other eyewitness accounts you read about in the chapter? Describe one of these accounts.

_____
_____
_____
_____
_____
_____
_____
_____
_____
_____
_____
_____
_____
_____
_____
_____
_____
_____

ENRICHMENT ACTIVITY

Compare and contrast the impact that the 1963 fire had on Cordova with the impact that the 1968 flood had on Fairbanks. How was it similar? How was it different? Write a short essay with supporting facts from Chapters 33 and 34.

LEARN MORE

Learn more about how floods form by visiting http://kids.nationalgeographic.com/explore/science/flood/#flood-house.jpg

UNIT 7: SOME LOW POINTS

LESSON 35: CONGRESSMEN DISAPPEAR

FACTS TO KNOW

Nicholas "Nick" Begich – Alaska congressman who disappeared along with U.S. House Majority Leader Hale Boggs, Begich aide Russell L. Brown and their pilot during a flight to Juneau in 1972

Don Jonz – Pilot who flew the plane that was lost in 1972 with U.S. Congressman Nick Begich on board

COMPREHENSION QUESTIONS

1) Why did Nick Begich and Hale Boggs decide to fly to Juneau in October 1972?
They left Anchorage early that day bound for Juneau to attend a Democratic fund-raiser. Begich was up for reelection and Boggs, a close personal friend, was helping him muster votes around the state. (Page 350)

2) Describe the search effort for the Cessna 310.
Search planes were in the sky within 90 minutes of the Federal Aviation Administration reporting the six-passenger aircraft had failed to land in Juneau. A U.S. Coast Guard searched and the Elmendorf Air Force Base dispatched three planes. Hundreds of boats from Cordova searched around Prince William Sound. Searchers selflessly flew in hair-raising weather conditions as hundreds of eyes looked for four needles in a 24,000-square-mile haystack. But none of the efforts found the missing plane. (Pages 352-355)

3) How did this search make history? What made the search difficult?
It was the longest aerial search in Alaska's history. Bad weather including milkshake-thick clouds, extreme turbulence, high winds and marble-size rain drops that could lead to extreme icing conditions made it difficult for search crews to navigate the massive search area. (Page 352)

4) When did the search officially end? What was the conclusion?
The search was called off on Nov. 24 as fresh snowfalls began covering the landscape. NTSB investigators later concluded that, "poor weather conditions not conducive to visual flight procedures was a critical factor in the crash." But they also said the plane would have to be found and examined before the true cause of the accident could be known. The disappearance of that airplane still remains a mystery. (Pages 354-356)

5) What other mystery was discovered after the search?
Another mystery also surrounded this incident. Newspapers reported that Jonz's employees had found the emergency locator beacon that was thought to be in the missing Cessna on their boss' desk at his Fairbanks office. They also found all the survival kits known to them were untouched still in Fairbanks. (Page 356)

DISCUSSION QUESTION

(Discuss this question with your teacher or write your answer in essay form below. Use additional paper if necessary.)

What conspiracies emerged about the plane's disappearance?

_____
_____
_____
_____
_____
_____
_____
_____
_____
_____
_____
_____
_____
_____
_____
_____
_____

TIME TO REVIEW

Review Chapters 29-35 of your book before moving on the Unit Review. See how many questions you can answer without looking at your book.

UNIT 6: SOME HIGHLIGHTS
UNIT 7: SOME LOW POINTS

REVIEW LESSONS 29-32

Write down what you remember about:

Cordova – *Small town in Prince William Sound that used the idea of an iceworm to combat mid-winter doldrums and draw tourists to town*

Iceworm – *Tiny black worms that avoid the sun and spend their lives in glacial ice*

Ohmer Waer – *Hotel manager in Cordova who had the idea of creating an "iceworm"*

Pachyderm – *Thick-skinned, hoofed mammal such as an elephant*

Annabelle – *Elephant that arrived in Anchorage in 1966*

Alaska Zoo – *Anchorage zoo started by Sammye Seawell, caretaker of Annabelle*

Homer – *City overlooking Kachemak Bay on the Kenai Peninsula*

General Mills – *National company that offered a program to exchange coupons for household items*

Dorothy Page – *Secretary of Aurora Dog Mushers Club who had the idea for an annual Iditarod Trail race*

Joe Redington Sr. – *Veteran dog musher who became known as the "father of the Iditarod"*

Iditarod Trail – *Historic trail that runs from Seward to Nome; the annual race runs from Willow to Nome*

Dick Wilmarth – *Gold miner who won the 1973 Iditarod Trail Race*

Prince William Sound – *Cordova, devastated by fire in May 1963, is located on this sound in the Gulf of Alaska on the east side of the Kenai Peninsula*

Kennecott Copper Mines – *At one time it was the largest copper mine in the world until it closed in 1938*

Chena River – *Fairbanks river that flooded in August 1967*

Fairbanks – *Large city in the interior of Alaska that experienced massive flooding in the summer of 1967*

Flood Control Act of 1968 – *Largest federal civil works program in the state, created to prevent future flooding in the Fairbanks area*

Nicholas "Nick" Begich – *Alaska congressman who disappeared along with U.S. House Majority Leader Hale Boggs, Begich aide Russell L. Brown and their pilot during a flight to Juneau in 1972*

Don Jonz – *Pilot who flew the plane that was lost in 1972 with U.S. Congressman Nick Begich on board*

Fill in the blanks:

1) "Get me something that will make *headlines* and sell papers," the editor of the Klondike Nugget told newsman *E.J. White*. As he pondered what sort of news might attract readers, a huge *storm* hit the Canadian gold-rush town. That's when a great idea hit the newsman. He announced that new creatures had emerged after the storm: *ice worms.*

2) Residents of *Cordova* rallied around an idea to make an *Iceworm* and have a celebration to shake off the winter blues.

3) Although many people believe *ice worms* are fantasy, they do, indeed, exist and were first discovered in 1887 on Alaska's Muir *Glacier*. The tiny black *worms* avoid the sun and spend their lives in *glacial ice*.

4) Annabelle, born in *India* in 1964, was the first *pachyderm/elephant* in Alaska since the ice age. It all started when *Jack Snyder* saw an ad for a Chiffon toilet paper contest for grocers in 1966. The company announced: "$3,000 or *a baby elephant*" to the winner. The Anchorage grocer won the contest and startled the tissue paper executives when he said, "I'll take *the elephant*."

5) The *Alaska Children's Zoo*, located on land adjacent to Sammye Seawell's ranch, opened in 1969 with *Annabelle* and other donated animals. The 30-acre park's name changed to *Alaska Zoo* in June 1980 and served as a star attraction to draw thousands of visitors to see various Alaska animals. A female *African elephant* named Maggie joined *Annabelle* as a companion in 1983.

6) Something magical happened at America's farthest-north zoo when trainers put a *paintbrush* into *Annabelle's* trunk in 1991. She started *splattering brush strokes across canvas and created paintings* in front of cheering visitors. Her *paintings* raised several hundred thousand dollars for the zoo.

7) Following the city of *Homer's* incorporation in 1964, the city issued a monthly check to the *fire department* for operations, fuel and maintenance. But when the need for a new *fire truck* arose in 1969, the city didn't have the money to buy one.

8) *Homer* residents turned to *Betty Crocker* after they learned about a promotion offered by *General Mills*. The nationally known company offered a program where people could turn in their *coupons* for large household items.

9) *Dorothy Page*, secretary of the Aurora Dog Mushers Club, thought a *sled dog race* on the historic *Iditarod Trail* – which originally began in *Seward* during the gold rush days and stretched to Knik, then through the gold camp of Iditarod and eventually to *Nome* – might revitalize a longtime Alaska tradition.

10) *Dorothy Page* talked to veteran musher *Joe Redington Sr.* about her idea. His response, "*I think that's a great idea!*" has been echoed by hundreds of *mushers* from all parts of Alaska and the world ever since.

11) On March 3, *1973*, amid the cheers of hundreds of well-wishers, 34 *mushers* left *Anchorage* headed for *Nome* in pursuit of not only a dream, but also $50,000 in prize money pledged by *Joe Redington Sr*. Dick *Wilmarth* crossed the finish line first and collected $12,000 in prize money.

12) The city of *Cordova* took a hit in 1938 when the *Kennecott copper mines* closed down. The *railroad* was abandoned and the *rails* sold for scrap. *Cordova* had another resource to fall back on – *fishing and canning fish, clams and crab* provided employment for the people who stayed with the town.

13) Then, on May 2, *1963*, it faced one of its greatest challenges. *Cordova*'s residents awoke in the early hours to find a major *fire* sweeping through their town. The *fire* did not stop until 14 *downtown buildings* had been destroyed and many more damaged, including City Hall and the fire department.

14) With the spirit and enthusiasm of pioneers past, *Cordova*'s citizens knuckled down and *rebuilt* their town. But this time they used different *building materials* – *concrete block* buildings replaced wooden frames.

15) While many *Fairbanks* residents were in the midst of the Alaska Purchase Centennial, celebrating the *U.S.* purchase of Alaska from *Russia* in *1867*, water from the *Chena* River was steadily rising as 3.34 inches of rain fell on the city.

16) In order to escape the waist-high flood waters, *Sandy Vernon* and her husband felt their way through water covering the *railroad tracks* in pitch black conditions not knowing that the water was washing away the *gravel underneath the ties*.

17) The flood put *Fairbanks* and Nenana under as much as 9 *feet* of water. *Seven* people died, and damage was estimated at *$200* million, according to the *Anchorage Daily News*.

18) The disappearance of Alaska's U.S. Congressman *Nicholas "Nick" Begich* on Oct. 16, 1972, sparked the most *intensive search* for an aircraft in Alaska's history. *Search planes* were in the sky within 90 minutes of the Federal Aviation Administration reporting the six-passenger aircraft had failed to land in *Juneau*.

19) The longest *aerial search* in Alaska's history finally was called off on *Nov. 24* as fresh snowfalls began covering the landscape. During its record-breaking *39 days*, searchers traced down *88 leads or sightings*, flew more than *3,600 hours* and covered more than *325,000* square miles at a cost of nearly *$1 million*.

20) Another *mystery* also surrounded this incident. Newspapers reported that pilot *Don Jonz's* employees had found the *emergency locator beacon* that was thought to be in the missing *Cessna* on their boss' desk at his Fairbanks office. They also found all the *survival kits* known to them untouched in Fairbanks.

Some Low Points
Word Search Key
Please find the words in the list below

CORDOVA
FLAMES
FLOOD
BOATS
SALVATION ARMY
NICK BEGICH
SEARCH
CONGRESSMEN
DISAPPEAR

FIRE
CATASTROPHE
FAIRBANKS
NATIONAL GUARD
REFUGEES
CESSNA
AIRPLANES
BEACON

EXPLOSION
FIREFIGHTERS
SLUDGY WATER
CHENA RIVER
DISASTER
JUNEAU
EMERGENCY LOCATOR
CIVIL AIR PATROL

UNIT 6: SOME HIGHLIGHTS
UNIT 7: SOME LOW POINTS

UNIT TEST

Choose *three* of the following questions to answer in paragraph form. Use as much detail as possible to completely answer the question.

1) Which two people used the idea of an Iceworm to create a buzz in Cordova? Summarize how they did this? What annual festival does Cordova celebrate surrounding the Iceworm?

2) How did the first pachyderm in Alaska since the ice age come to Anchorage? What special talent did she have? What organization did she inspire in the 1960s?

3) How did the community of Homer receive a new firetruck for their town in the late 1960s? Include details about who was involved in the process and how it all came together. What did the fire chief at the time say about this story? What did it represent for their city?

4) What great race was born in the 1960s-1970s? Why was the race put on hold after its first race in 1967? Who won in 1973? Why did he have an advantage over many of his competitors?

5) Compare and contrast the impact that the 1963 fire had on Cordova with the impact that the 1968 flood had on Fairbanks. How was it similar? How was it different? Include details about each event in your answer.

6) How did the search for U.S. Congressman Nicholas "Nick" Begich make history? What mysteries surrounded his disappearance? What conspiracies arose surrounding this event?

_____
_____
_____
_____
_____
_____
_____
_____
_____
_____
_____
_____
_____

TEACHER NOTES ABOUT THIS UNIT

TEACHER NOTES ABOUT THIS UNIT

NOTE TO TEACHERS/PARENTS

Chapters 36-39 in the section Mass Murder in the North, pages 359-400, contain details about historical murder cases that may be too graphic for some students/classrooooms. Teachers can elect to assign these chapters for extra reading.

Please note: There are no workbook lessons 36-39 for these chapters.

This photograph is from the Alaska Territorial Department of Education classroom at Gustavus in Southeast Alaska taken in 1931.

Gustavus, which was formerly known as Strawberry Point, is less than 100 years old. But Tlingits used the area for fishing, berry picking and other activities.

The first settlers arrived in 1914, but they did not stay. The first permanent homestead was established in 1917, when Abraham Lincoln Parker moved his family there.

Sources say many strawberries still may be found in the area.

UNIT 8: 25 YEARS IN THE NEWS

LESSON 40: 1960s IN THE NEWS

Summarize each event:

1) **1961: Survival story tops the news**
The survival story of postal clerk William C. Waters, a Kentucky tourist lost for 69 days in the subarctic wilderness northeast of Fairbanks, was the No. 1 story for 1961. When two moose hunters finally found him sitting along a creek many miles north on Aug. 27, Waters was about 100 pounds lighter and nearly starved. (Page 401)

2) **1962: Japanese ship seized**
Gov. William A. Egan's dramatic seizure of two Japanese catcher boats and the 1,772-ton herring fleet mother ship, the Banshu Manu, off Uganik Bay in Shelikof Strait in mid-April made the No. 1 news story of 1962. (Page 402)

3) **1963: Crash victims survive more than a month in the wilderness**
The No. 1 story for 1963 was the amazing survival of 21-year-old Helen Klaben and Ralph Flores after their plane crashed in the Canadian wilderness while flying from Fairbanks to California. Flores lost 51 pounds, Klaben lost 45 and had the toes of her right food amputated due to frostbite. She wrote about the experience in 1964 in "Hey, I'm Alive," which later was made into a movie. (Page 403)

4) **1966: St. Michael's Cathedral burns**
The burning of St. Michael's topped the news in 1966. On the morning of Jan. 2, 1966, fire destroyed the beloved St. Michael's Cathedral, reported the Seattle Times. The 119-year-old Russian Orthodox church was a favorite landmark with Alaskans and tourists of all faiths. (Page 404)

5) **1967: State motto**
The state motto, "North to the Future," became official on Oct. 1, 1967, by an act passed by the Alaska Legislature, which also directed that the motto be put on automobile license plates. (Page 405)

6) **1968: Sen. Ted Stevens**
Alaska Gov. Walter J. Hickel appointed Anchorage attorney Theodore "Ted" Stevens to the U.S. Senate on Dec. 24, 1968, to fill the seat left vacant when E. L. "Bob" Bartlett died in office on Dec. 11. (Page 406)

7) 1969: Alaskans receive first live feed from satellite

Alaskans had a front-row seat to watch astronaut Neil Armstrong plant the first footsteps on the moon on July 20, 1969, when the first live satellite telecast came to Anchorage. Following that historic step, Alaska leapt forward with satellites providing television, long-distance telephones and other high-speed communications of the day. (Page 407)

8) 1969: Gravel dreams up Dome City

Alaska's Demotractic U.S. Senator Mike Gravel proposed a never-built "Denali City" development above the Tokositna River in 1969. As he envisioned it, the $800-million, climate-controlled Teflon-domed city across the Knik Arm from Anchorage would have contained malls, condos, a golf course, hotels and a conference center. Gravel sought federal funds for his dream, which never materialized. (Page 408)

DISCUSSION QUESTION

(Discuss this question with your teacher or write your answer in essay form below. Use additional paper if necessary.)

Which story from the 1960s was most interesting to you and why?

_____
_____
_____
_____
_____
_____
_____
_____
_____
_____
_____
_____
_____

ENRICHMENT ACTIVITY

Would you like to learn more about what happened in the news during the 1960s? See if you can find an interesting story about something that happened in Alaska during the 1960s by searching online or visiting the library. Write a short summary about the story and present it to your class.

LEARN MORE

See a beautiful satellite picture of Alaska by visiting http://www.livescience.com/37560-alaska-from-space.html

UNIT 8: 25 YEARS IN THE NEWS

LESSON 41: 1970s IN THE NEWS

Summarize each event:

1) 1971: Alaskans watch 1971 NFC championship game live
Television broadcasting pioneer August "Augie" Hiebert broke new ground on Jan. 3, 1971, when he treated Alaskans to their first-ever live satellite broadcast of a professional football game from the U.S. mainland. Alaskans watching KTVA Channel 11 saw the Dallas Cowboys beat the San Francisco 49ers by a score of 17 to 10 in that 1971 National Football Conference championship game. (Page 409)

2) 1972: Benny Benson dies
John Ben "Benny" Benson, the Aleut who designed the Alaska state flag in 1926, died in a Kodiak hospital at the age of 58 on July 2, 1972. His design, which he created for an American Legion contest for schoolchildren, consists of eight gold stars on a field of blue that represent the Big Dipper and the North Star. (Page 411)

3) 1974: Ernest Guening dies
After a long and illustrious career serving Alaska as a politician and statesman, Ernest Gruening died on June 26, 1974, at the age of 87. He served as Alaska's territorial governor, an activist for statehood and U.S. senator. Gruening also was one of the first to fight for the rights and wellbeing of Alaska's Native people. His ashes were scattered on a mountaintop above Juneau. (Page 411)

4) 1975: Wien Air Alaska crashes near Gambell
Thirty-one people were on board a Wien Air Alaska Fairchild F-27 when it slammed into the side of Seuvokuk Mountain near Gambell on St. Lawrence Island on Aug. 30, 1975. Ten died, but 21 lived through the flaming crash – most survived due to the heroic efforts of then-Alaska State Trooper Gilbert Pelawook. The National Transportation and Safety Board determined fog was heavy that day and the crew failed to follow instrument approach procedures. (Page 412)

5) 1976: Molly Hootch case
The lawsuit of Tobeluk v. Lind, known by most as the Molly Hootch case, was settled in 1976. A detailed decree provided for the establishment of a high school program in all 126 villages covered by the litigation, unless people in the village decided against a local program. Prior to this, children who wanted to go to high school had no choice but to leave their villages. (Page 413)

6) 1978: D-2 Lands hot topic

The Alaska Native Claims Settlement Act required the Secretary of the Interior to withdraw as many as 80 million acres of federally owned land in Alaska for inclusion in four national conservation systems: parks, forests, wildlife refuges and wild and scenic river areas. President Jimmy Carter soon designated 56 million of those acres as national monuments under the Antiquities Act. (Page 415)

7) 1979: Old Believers become U.S. citizens

Eighty-six Russian Old Believers who found refuge and religious freedom in Alaska in the late 1960s became U.S. citizens on Monday, April 30, 1979, on the Kenai Peninsula. The men, women and children renounced allegiance to any foreign nation in the Anchor Point school gymnasium. Old Believers separated from the Russian Orthodox Church after 1666, as a protest against church reforms. (Page 417)

8) 1979: Progress brings high prices

For Bush Alaska, the 1970s brought changes like improved airstrips, new high schools, clinics and city buildings. Electric bills, fuel oil bills and telephone bills added up in communities that historically relied on subsistence lifestyles. (Page 417)

DISCUSSION QUESTION

(Discuss this question with your teacher or write your answer in essay form below. Use additional paper if necessary.)

Which story from the 1970s was more interesting to you and why?

_____
_____
_____
_____
_____

ENRICHMENT ACTIVITY

Would you like to learn more about what happened in the news during the 1970s? See if you can find an interesting story about something that happened in Alaska during the 1970s by searching online or visiting the library. Write a short summary about the story and present it to your class.

LEARN MORE

Read about more news from the 1970s by visiting http://www.akhistorycourse.org/south-central-alaska/1970-1980-the-land-and-its-uses

UNIT 8: 25 YEARS IN THE NEWS

LESSON 42: 1980s IN THE NEWS

Summarize each event:

1) 1980: ANILCA passed
Congress passed the Alaska National Interest Lands Conservation Act on Nov. 12, 1980, and President Jimmy Carter signed it into law on Dec. 2 that year. The act provided varying degrees of special protection to more than 150 million acres of land in Alaska, doubling the size of the country's national park and refuge system and tripling the amount of land designated as wilderness. It was called the most significant land conservation measure in the history of the nation. (Page 419)

2) 1982: First PFD checks issues
The state Legislature passed a law authorizing equal dividend payments to all six-month residents. The first Permanent Fund dividend checks were distributed on June 14, 1982, in the amount of $1,000 to all Alaskans who had resided in Alaska for six months. The Legislature paid it with surplus oil revenues, not with Permanent Fund income. The residency requirement for eligibility was changed to 12 months in 1990. (Page 420)

3) 1983: Time zones changed
Time zones shifted to include all Alaska, except western-most Aleutian Islands, to one zone called Alaska Standard Time in 1983. It made most Alaska time one hour earlier than Pacific Standard Time, which helped businesses and the military communicate most of the day within and outside of the state. (Page 421)

4) 1984: Respected Native leader dies
Alaska Native leader Frank Peratrovich died on Jan. 4, 1984, at the age of 88. He was one of the first Natives elected to the Territorial Legislature, one of two Natives on the Alaska Statehood Committee and the only Native at the Constitutional Convention in 1955-56. Peratrovich, who came from the small Tlingit community of Klawock in Southeast, was the second Native to become president of the Alaska Senate following statehood. (Page 422)

5) 1984: Alaska celebrates 25 years of statehood
Alaskans celebrated the state's 25th anniversary throughout 1984, including at a banquet in the Wood Center at the University of Alaska Fairbanks that January. A wall-size reproduction of the stamp that commemorated the special year was at the head of the table. (Page 423)

6) 1984: Russians seize Homer ship

The five-man crew of the 115-foot Homer-based supply ship Frieda-K thought they were in American waters when a crew from a Russian military ship arrested them. The Russian soldiers took the Homer seamen to an abandoned military barracks in the Siberian city of Provideniya. Eight days later, the Homer men were handed over to the U.S. Coast Guard by a Soviet warship in a mid-ocean rendezvous west of Nome. (Page 424)

DISCUSSION QUESTION

(Discuss this question with your teacher or write your answer in essay form below. Use additional paper if necessary.)

Which story from the 1980s was most interesting to you and why?

_____
_____
_____
_____
_____
_____
_____
_____
_____
_____
_____
_____
_____
_____

TIME TO REVIEW

Review Chapters 40-42 of your book before moving on the Unit Review. See how many questions you can answer without looking at your book.

Alaskans celebrated the Last Frontier's 25th anniversary as a state throughout 1984. Picnics, ceremonies and festivities were planned and many communities, like Juneau seen in this photograph, filled the northern skies with fireworks.

UNIT 8: 25 YEARS IN THE NEWS

REVIEW LESSONS 40-42

Fill in the blanks:

1) **1961: Survival story tops news**
The survival story of <u>postal clerk</u> William C. Waters, a <u>Kentucky</u> tourist lost for 69 days in the subarctic wilderness northeast of <u>Fairbanks,</u> was the No. 1 story for 1961. When two <u>moose hunters</u> finally found him sitting along a creek many miles north on Aug. 27, about 100 pounds lighter and nearly <u>starved</u>, Waters became the subject of widespread national and international publicity.

2) **1967: State Motto**
The state motto, "<u>North to the Future</u>," became official on Oct. 1, 1967, by an act passed by the Alaska Legislature, which also directed that the motto be put on <u>automobile license plates.</u>

3) **1968: Sen. Ted Stevens**
Alaska <u>Gov. Walter J. Hickel</u> appointed Anchorage attorney Ted Stevens to the U.S. Senate on Dec. 24, 1968, to fill the seat left vacant when <u>E. L. "Bob" Bartlett</u> died in office on Dec. 11.

4) **1969: Alaskans receive first live feed from satellite**
Alaskans had a front-row seat to watch astronaut <u>Neil Armstrong</u> plant the first footsteps on the moon on <u>July 20, 1969</u>, when the first live satellite telecast came to <u>Anchorage.</u> Legendary Alaska broadcast pioneer August G. "Augie" Hiebert birthed television in Alaska with KTVA. Following that historic step, Alaska leapt forward with satellites providing <u>television, long- distance telephones</u> and other high-speed communications of the day.

5) **1974: Ernest Gruening dies**
After a long and illustrious career serving Alaska as a politician and statesman, Ernest Gruening died on June 26, 1974, at the age of 87. He served as Alaska's <u>territorial governor</u>, an activist for <u>statehood</u> and U.S. senator. Gruening also was one of the first to fight for the rights and wellbeing of Alaska's <u>Native people</u>. His ashes were scattered on a mountaintop above Juneau.

6) **1976: Molly Hootch case**
The suit of Tobeluk v. Lind, known by most as the Molly Hootch case, was settled in 1976. A detailed decree provided for the establishment of a *high school* program in all 126 *villages* covered by the litigation, unless people in the *village* decided against a local program. Prior to this, children who wanted to go to *high school* had no choice but to leave their *villages*.

7) **1980: ANILCA passed**
Congress passed the *Alaska National Interest Lands Conservation Act* on Nov. 12, 1980, and President *Jimmy Carter* signed it into law on Dec. 2 that year. The act provided varying degrees of special protection to more than 150 million acres of land in Alaska, doubling the size of the country's *national park and refuge system* and tripling the amount of land designated as *wilderness*. It was called the most significant *land conservation* measure in the history of the nation.

8) **1983: Time zones changed**
Time zones shifted to include all Alaska, except *western-most Aleutian Islands,* to one zone called Alaska *Standard Time* in 1983. It made most Alaska time one hour *earlier* than Pacific Standard Time, which helped businesses and the military communicate most of the day within and outside of the state.

9) **1984: Alaska celebrates 25 years of statehood**
Alaskans celebrated the state's 25th anniversary throughout 1984, including at a *banquet* in the Wood Center at the *University of Alaska Fairbanks* that January. A wall-size reproduction of the *stamp* that commemorated the special year was at the head of the table.

UNIT 8: 25 YEARS IN THE NEWS

UNIT TEST

Answer *all* of the following questions in paragraph form. Use as much detail as possible to completely answer the question.

1) Name at least three major news stories in Alaska from the 1960s. Why were each of these events important?

2) Name at least three major news stories in Alaska from the 1970s. Why were each of these events important?

3) Name at least three major news stories in Alaska from the 1980s. Why were each of these events important?

TEACHER NOTES ABOUT THIS UNIT

TEACHER NOTES

www.ingramcontent.com/pod-product-compliance
Lightning Source LLC
Chambersburg PA
CBHW082126230426
43671CB00015B/2815